POLICY CREATIVITY: NEW PERSPECTIVES

POLICY CREATIVITY: NEW PERSPECTIVES

STUART NAGEL (EDITOR)

Nova Science Publishers, Inc.
New York

Senior Editors: Susan Boriotti and Donna Dennis
Coordinating Editor: Tatiana Shohov
Office Manager: Annette Hellinger
Graphics: Wanda Serrano
Book Production: Matthew Kozlowski, Jonathan Rose and Jennifer Vogt
Circulation: Raymond Davis, Cathy DeGregory, Ave Maria Gonzalez
           and Andre Tillman
Communications and Acquisitions: Serge P. Shohov

Library of Congress Cataloging-in-Publication Data
Available Upon Request

ISBN 1-59033-240-7.

Copyright © 2002 by Nova Science Publishers, Inc.
           227 Main Street, Suite 100
           Huntington, New York 11743
           Tele. 631-424-NOVA (6682)   Fax 631-425-5933
           E Mail: Novascience@earthlink.net
           www.novapublishers.com

Printed in the United States of America

CONTENTS

PART ONE:

CAUSES AND CORRELATES OF CREATIVITY

Chapter 1

CREATIVITY AS AN EFFECT OF USEFUL TOOLS

This article is an extension of the article entitled "Creativity as Cause and Effect" in the Spring 2000 issue of *Creativity Plus*.

That addition discussed two effects of creativity consisting of (1) social changes, such as e-mail, and (2) individual benefits and costs, such as income received by envy encourages. That article also discussed two causes of creativity consisting of (1) public policies, like free speech and press, and (2) individual traits, such as ego involvement and being middle class.

This addition deals with creativity as an effect of useful tools. One could also say that this article deals with the role of individual facilitators in stimulating creativity. Those facilitators include the following:

1. HOW-TO-DO-IT LISTS. Such lists have appeared in the first two issues of *Creativity Plus* under such titles as (1) "Generating Creativity Ideas," (2) "Sources of Goals, Policies, and Relations, (3) "Creative Problem Solving," and (4) "Bopping Out of the Box."

2. INSPIRATIONAL AIDS. These include audio and visual aids like those described in the article entitled, "Inspiration Aids" in the Spring 2000 issue. To find an ideal combination of audio and visual aids, one can experiment with whatever device is available for sampling video and audio tapes and disks.

3. OTHER PEOPLE. Those people can be pushing, facilitating, or pulling people, as described in the article on "Generating Creative Ideas" in the Autumn-Winter issue. They might also be people who are sexually attractive, as described in the article on "Creativity and Sex" in the Spring issue.

4. CREATIVITY AIDING SOFTWARE. The most appropriate software might be spread sheet-based with goals on the columns, alternatives on the rows, and relations between the alternatives and the goals in the cells. The object is to find an alternative that gets the highest total score

on all the foals collectively, on certain goals, or on both the conservative and liberal goals.

5. SLEEP, FOOD, EXERCISE, AND HEALTH AIDS. All in moderation. Too much sleep means missed opportunities to be creative. Too little sleep can interfere with creativity and can even be hallucinatory. Too much food is sleep-producing. Too little food may weaken one's body and mind. Too much exercise can be exhausting. Too little exercise can be stultifying.

6. FLEXIBLE ORGANIZATION. This means developing a reasonably firm schedule of constructive creativity activities, but with flexibility for sleeping, and eating, and diversions that generate creativity.

This series of articles dealing with the causes and effects of creativity is being developed for a book called, *Creativity on the Cutting Edge*. The manuscript was recently completed, but a publisher has not yet been found.

Chapter 2

TESTING FOR CREATIVITY AND
RELATED PSYCHOLOGY CONCEPTS

The purpose of this short article is to discuss how one might devise a test for creativity, and how such a test might differ from related tests for knowledge, skills, general intelligence, verbal intelligence, quantitative intelligence, memory, common sense, personality, and motivation.

I. RELATED CONCEPTS

A. Knowledge, Skills, and Intelligence

A *knowledge* test might ask, "When did Columbus discover America?" or "How much is 2 plus 2?" More advanced knowledge tests can be developed. To validate a knowledge test, one can come up with a battery of many questions and give them to a random sample on adults or some other age group. If 100% get the right answer, then that is rather elementary knowledge. If 0% get the right answer, that is rather advanced or unknown knowledge. Each question can be given a score based on the percentage of those who know the right answer in order to have different degrees of difficulty.

Such a knowledge test might be considered rather useless because it is too general. Instead we probably want to have knowledge tests for specific subject matters. That would include knowledge tests for receiving a medical, law, or CPA license. It would include the knowledge tests in specific academic disciplines which are part of the Graduate Record Examination. It would include the specific knowledge tests that are given by the National Assessment for Educational Progress (NAEP) of the U.S. Department of Education to those who are 14 year old graduates of elementary school, 18 year old graduates of high school, 22 year old graduates of college, or 40 year old adults.

Closely related are *skills* tests. They are generally based on experience, rather than just on reading books or listening to lectures. This includes a driver's licenses test, a typing test, or a test to be a carpenter. Some tests involve both skills and knowledge which is true of the usual driver's license test.

Intelligence is the ability to learn, whereas knowledge is information that has already been learned. How does one measure intelligence? There are numerous fields of knowledge and numerous skills. Intelligence, though, seems to be basically either verbal or quantitative. The typical verbal intelligence test may emphasize vocabulary or reading comprehension. Those tests are frequently defective because they heavily measure knowledge, rather than ability to learn. Likewise, a typical quantitative intelligence test may involve math problems. They may also over-emphasize prior knowledge, rather than pure ability to learn quantitative reasoning.

A pure *verbal intelligence* test might involve giving the test taker 10 nonsense words. Each word could consist of four letters randomly put together. The words would include nouns, verbs, adjectives, and adverbs. The test taker would then be given five different sentences to translate using those ten words. If the test taker translates all five sentences accurately, then he or she has demonstrated the ability to learn words and a pseudo language. If the test taker can not accurately translate any of the sentences, then that seems to indicate a lack of verbal intelligence or verbal ability to learn.

A pure *quantitative intelligence* test might involve explaining to the test-taker that we have a ten-based numbering system that goes from 0 to 9, and then the next number involves a combination of 1 and 0 in order to make a ten. There is no symbol in the Arabic numbering system for a ten unlike the Roman numbering system in which an X represents a ten. In order to show that we are in the tens, we put a number in the second column. After explaining that to the test taker, he or she is then asked to develop combinations of numbers 0, 1, 2, and 3 for a numbering system that is based on four rather than ten. That means the number four is shown by writing a 10. Further explanation may be needed. The test taker is then asked to write out (using the four-based numbering system) the corresponding numbers for 7, 11, 15, and 25. If the test taker gets all five correct, then he or she has demonstrated an ability to deal with number concepts that he is not likely to have mastered before. Thus this could be a better test of quantitative ability to learn than the traditional math-based quantitative tests.

B. Memory and Common Sense

Memory is closely related to ability to learn. One cannot learn anything of lasting value without being able to remember. Thus it may be difficult to devise a test that is solely for intelligence or ability to learn and not partly for memory. One can develop a memory test that is highly but not completely divorced from intelligence. Such a test would involve reading to the test taker a list of five unconnected words and then asking them to be repeated. Then try six words, seven, and so on. The test could also use numbers like five numbers, six, and so on. If the test taker can fairly consistently remember ten words or ten numbers, then that is good memory. There may be an unavoidable element of intelligence also present because the test taker may be quickly developing an acronym or a mnemonic.

Common sense is difficult to test for. If by common sense we mean common knowledge, then this is a knowledge test. If by common sense we mean ability to learn, then this is an intelligence test. Common sense may refer to something that is different from either knowledge or intelligence. The term is sometimes used to refer to practical knowledge, but that is getting at the subject matter. Knowing carpentry is practical knowledge, but is not considered common sense. If a person is shown a hammer, a screwdriver, some nails, and some screws (who has never seen them before), then it is common sense to figure out that the hammer is used with the nails and the screwdriver is used with the screws. It might however be difficult to find test takers who have never seen these tools. A good test distinguishes between levels of ability among test takers.

For a common sense test to be meaningful, it has to be separate from knowledge and intelligence. Perhaps such a test might involve a question like "If A = B and B = C, then what does C equal?" If the test taker answers D or "I don't know," then he or she seems to lack common sense. If the test taker says, "C equals A," then that shows moderate reasoning. If the test taker says, "C equals A, and C equals B," then that shows even better reasoning. Common sense seems to involve ability to reason, but with regard to very simple matters, and not with regard to complicated syllogisms.

C. Personality and Motivation

If we are talking about psychological testing related to creativity, then we should also talk about personality and motivation. Those concepts may be even more closely related to creativity. Personality can be classified in a variety of ways. Perhaps the most relevant classification is whether one has a positive or can-do personality, rather than a negative or can't-do personality. When both kinds of people are faced with a situation calling for creativity, the can-do personality is more likely to succeed even if the two people are equal on relevant knowledge, skills, intelligence, memory, and common sense. This may be true even if the can't-do personality is mildly superior on those other characteristics. The area of creativity may be more subject to self-fulfilling prophecies than almost any subject about which one might predict the future.

Closely related to having a positive can-do personality is the personality characteristic of perseverance. It is quite possible that Thomas Edison was really not very creative when it came to inventing the light bulb. He had to experiment with approximately 700 different filaments, gases, and containers before he arrived at the right combination in which a tungsten filament was the key element. Perhaps ten years before, some unknown person was on the track of discovering the light bulb, but quit after the 600th trial or maybe after the tenth trial. That person might have discovered the light bulb on the 11th trial and thus he would have been in that sense more creative than Edison.

Another highly relevant personality characteristic is whether a person has a collaborative personality or an intellectually paranoid personality. Those are opposite extremes with degrees in between. The collaborative personality is like John Kennedy who worked well with others. He is given credit for being highly creative when much of his creativity was stimulated by working with others who are sometimes referred to as the best and the brightest. The intellectually paranoid personality is like Richard Nixon who preferred to be surrounded by yes-men who would not upstage him. As a result, he may have missed a lot of opportunities to be creative. Perhaps his greatest creativity was in the area of welfare reform where he was advised by Democrat Daniel Patrick Moynihan. Nixon abandoned him in order to appease southern senators into blocking Nixon's impeachment.

Maybe even more important than relevant personality characteristics is motivation, although many of these concepts overlap. Motivation in this context refers to being driven to find creative solutions to specific problems. Otherwise, things that one highly values will be lost. Edison did not highly value having light at night. He did highly value his ego. He would therefore artificially motivate himself by announcing a few months in advance that he would hold a press conference to demonstrate the light bulb which he had not yet invented. For the next few months, he would go with little sleep and much motivation to show light from a light bulb at midnight in the winter to a set of previously skeptical reporters, scientists, and other people whose respect Edison valued.

Motivation is a link between creativity and both Marx and Freud. Marxists might say that a society like Tsarist Russia with sharply divided economic classes of rich and poor is not so likely to be creative. Poor people are too busy struggling for food, shelter, and clothing. Rich people may be too satiated to be motivated to be creative. Karl Marx liked the U.S. and the Netherlands partly because they were relatively middle class societies with lots of upward mobility and thus more stimulating to creativity.

Freudians might say that creativity is partly due to a conscious or subconscious desire to impress members of the opposite sex or members of the same sex if that is one's sexual orientation. Thus, measuring sexuality could be considered as measuring a correlate or even a cause of creativity. This is not because estrogen or testosterone cause creativity. It is because if one is sexually dead, then one lacks the motivation to be creative in order to intellectually score.

II. TESTING FOR CREATIVITY

A. Creativity among Professors

Now we may be ready to talk about a test for creativity. One might say why did we waste time talking about these other concepts first? The answer is partly because these concepts are frequently confused with creativity and with each other. University professors may be highly knowledgeable, but only in their own fields. They may be highly intelligent, but not necessarily both verbal and quantitative. They may lack some skills like carpentry, sports, and social graces. They are reputed to lack streetwise common sense, whatever that is.

Professors are reputed to have lots of creativity, but that might be a bit questionable.

First, they tend to be creative only in their own field, and not necessarily have something that is called general creativity. General intelligence is both quantitative and verbal. General knowledge covers lots of subjects.

Second, if creativity means to be usefully innovative, then a lot of professors who do a lot of publishing might find it difficult to say that their publishing is creative. Much of it may not be very useful for improving how things are done or even for improving our understanding of causation. Much of it is a demonstration of methodological elegance.

Third, their publications may not be very innovative either if much of it involves presenting the same ideas that have been repeatedly published, although with a slight variation. Is it innovative, for example, if the publication shows the correlation between the background characteristics of voters and whether they vote Democratic or Republican in Illinois in 1996, when we have seen that kind of research in numerous states, cities, years, and elections?

Fourth, only 5% of the faculty at even major universities are reputed to write 95% of the books. This is sometimes referred to as the Babe Ruth syndrome where there have to be numerous strikeouts to hit a home run. Likewise universities need to tolerate less productive faculty in order to have the more productive ones. It is difficult when hiring and even when giving tenure to know who the more productive or creative ones will be.

B. Creativity Testing

Back to measuring creativity. One frequently suggested way is to show the test taker a Rohrsach inkblot and ask him or her what he sees. If the test taker says a butterfly, then this is considered not very creative. If the test taker says the inkblot is Ross Perot's ears, that is more creative or more unusual. We could validate such a test by showing the same inkblot to 1,000 people. If the test taker says something that a high percentage also said, then this is not very creative. If, however, only 2% of the 1,000 say x, and the text taker says x, then that is creative. This is not a very good approach because people will quickly say wild things in order to appear to be creative, such as the inkblot looks like a rhinoceros dancing with a flea.

Perhaps the best way to measure creativity is not with any kind of a pencil-paper or interviewing test like a knowledge or intelligence test. Perhaps the best way is to ask the test taker what have you done that might be considered creative? Or what have you published, assuming publications indicate creativity, especially books. Or what have you composed, painted, sculptured, or otherwise designed for which there is a commercial market. Or what have you invented, discovered, or developed that might be considered innovatively useful. Questions like those might be much more meaningful in indicating a person's creativity.

There is considerable subjectivity in evaluating the answers. But the answers could be used to rank order people or to classify people as high, medium, or low even though such questions and answers would not be likely to generate a creativity quotient analogous to the traditional intelligence quotient.

A cynic, skeptic, or both might object on the grounds that such questions would not be meaningful to ask young people who have not yet established themselves. That seems to be a wrong response for two reasons. First, even five-year olds have probably done some creative things, although not necessarily at a Nobel Prize level. If five-year-olds can be creative then so can 25-year-olds. Second, if we wait until a person's lifetime has gone by to ask him or her what creative things they have done, by then the analysis may be too late to use for career counseling or for making hiring decisions.

C. Why Test for Creativity?

One might logically ask, "Why measure creativity?" It is useful to do so for the purpose of admitting students to graduate research in Ph.D. programs where they are expected to be productive scholars. Measuring creativity is useful for hiring university faculty or corporate executives. It is useful in research situations where one is attempting to determine what causes creativity or what improves creativity across different types of people or in before-after situations.

If creativity means being usefully innovative in diverse situations, then a past performance test does seem to be the most meaningful test for creativity. Such a test is not mutually exclusive with a pencil/paper test that involves drawing pictures or interpreting inkblots. None of these tests or concepts are mutually exclusive. They all overlap to some extent, and they involve reciprocal causation. For example, being highly motivated may cause successful creativity, but successful creativity feeds back and reinforces one's motivation. We could draw a matrix with all the variables on the top and on the left side. In the cells, we could indicate how each concept definitionally overlaps or reciprocally causes each other concept.

A five-person evaluating committee might be likely to agree that a certain person's past performance is indicative of high creativity. But they may not be likely to agree that his picture drawing or inkblot interpreting is indicative of high creativity in the sense of being both innovative and broadly useful. Thus a good way to deal with developing creativity questions or tests (and a good way of interpreting the results) is by a committee using some method of averaging their opinions.

As for the diversity of creativity, that may be less important than having a lot of it in one field. We do not expect much of anybody to be another Leonardo DaVinci or a Renaissance man. It is enough to be a Thomas Edison. He was only highly creative in matters of physics and engineering, but he never composed a Beethoven symphony or did a Rembrandt paintinq.

In conclusion, creativity is a highly important human characteristic. As just indicated, it leads to inventing printing presses, light bulbs, cures for diseases, great symphonies, and solutions to public policy problems. It is something that we should be seeking to measure. More important, however, is seeking to improve it even if we can not exactly measure it.

Creativity may be a bit like pornography was to Supreme Court Justice Potter Stewart. He said roughly, "I cannot measure pornography, but I know it when I see it, and I think it ought to be decreased." We may not be able to measure creativity, but we sort of know it when we see it, and it ought to be increased.

Chapter 3

CREATIVITY-AIDING SOFTWARE

The purpose of this article is to describe some aspects of creativity-aiding software in general, with particular emphasis on the package called "Policies/Goals Percentaging." That software relates public policies to goals in a spreadsheet format. It uses percentaging when the goals are measured on different dimensions and when working with allocation problems.

I. SPREADSHEET-BASED

Perhaps spreadsheet-based software is the kind of software that is most appropriate for stimulating creativity, especially policy creativity. Such software puts the goals to be achieved on the columns, the alternatives for achieving them on the rows.

Indicators of the relations between the alternatives and goals are put in the cells of the spreadsheet matrix. Those indicators can be numbers from 1 to 5 where 5 indicates the alternative is highly conducive to the goal, 4 indicates mildly conducive, 3 is neither conducive nor adverse, 2 is mildly adverse to the goal, and 1 indicates highly adverse.

To make the matrix more applicable to public policy creativity, one or more goal, columns can be devoted to conservative goals, and one or more to liberal goals. Likewise, one or more rows can be devoted to conservative alternatives, and one or more to liberal alternatives. One would expect the conservative alternatives to do well on the conservative goals, but not so well on the liberal goals. One would likewise expect the liberal alternatives to do well on the liberal goals, but not so well on the conservative goals.

The object of the software and that kind of matrix is to stimulate the user's creativity into thinking of a new alternative that will do well on both sets of goals. That is what we mean by a win-win or super-optimizing alternative.

II. ADVANTAGES OVER UNAIDED THINKING

One might ask how is the software helpful for finding such a win-win alternative, rather than just thinking about the problem. The software is a creativity-facilitator in the following ways:

1. The software causes the user to think more explicitly about what the conservative and liberal goals are.
2. It causes the user to also be more explicit about the conservative and liberal alternatives.
3. The user must in addition be more explicit about the relations between alternatives and goals.
4. The matrix clearly shows what thresholds the win-win alternatives have to exceed.
5. Changes can easily be made on the goals, alternatives, and relations to see how they affect the overall picture.
6. The matrix software approach causes the user to be more explicit in describing a win-win solution and how it relates to the conservative and liberal goals and alternatives.
7. The software can be used to allocate scarce resources in a win-win way, as contrasted to deciding among non-allocation alternatives.
8. The software can quantify relations and especially concepts like sensitivity analysis, threshold analysis, convergence analysis, and other ways of saying how close the second-place or other-place alternative is to the win-win alternative.
9. The software is especially good at keeping ideas well-organized when there are many goals, many alternatives, and/or many win-win proposals.
10. The same software can be used for predicting what alternative is likely to be adopted in light of various predictive criteria, as well as what alternative should be adopted in light of various normative criteria.
11. The software is excellent for teaching purposes because it enables the students to actively participate in the teaching process, rather than to just passively listen.
12. The software can effectively handle multi-dimensionality, whereby not all the goals are measured on 1-5 scales, but in diverse ways.
13. The software can handle missing information in various ways, although the main way is to indicate how much changes would have to occur in the data in order for a win-win proposal to be a loser.
14. The software can handle conflicting restraints by indicating how much a budget needs to expand, and then analyzing the alternatives for expanding the budget. It can also show what adjustments need to be made in minimums, maximums, relations, or other input data to be able

to simultaneously satisfy all the constraints and still have all the major sides come out ahead of their best initial expectations simultaneously.

III. WIN-WIN MENTIONS AND CREATIVITY-AIDING SOFTWARE

1. "Decision-Aiding software and the concept of super-optimal solutions would be attractive. I will use it in my lectures and demonstrations." *Ivan Grdesic, University of Zagreb, Croatia.*
2. "We are indeed interested in your work dealing with policy analysis, decision-aiding software, and super-optimizing solutions in the context of developmental policy and developmental countries." *Hidehiko Sazanmi, Director, United Nations Centre for Regional Development.*
3. "Easy to use program. Covers a complex topic well. Supporting print materials are very extensive." *Chuck Bilow, Evaluation from the Wisc-Ware Software Distribution System.*
4. "I am keen to look at the software with a view to using it with MBA students in particular." *Reviewer, Abacus Press.*
5. "Without question P/G% is the best of the available software. No other program is as versatile and powerful or as inexpensive." *Social Science Microcomputer Review, 1986.*

IV. FURTHER REFERENCES

For further details on creativity-aiding software, especially in the context of win-win analysis, see:

1. C+ Editors, "Foresight and Hindsight in Win-Win Analysis" in the Autumn 2000 Policy *Evaluation.*
2. "Using Microcomputers to Teach Policy Studies Substance" in the Spring 1997 *Policy Evaluation.*
3. S. Nagel, *Computer-Aided Decision Analysis: Theory and Applications,* (Quorum Books, 1993), 301 pages.
4. S. Nagel, *Decision-Aiding Software: Skills, Obstacles, and Applications,* (Macmillan, 1991), 320 pages.
5. S. Nagel, and Bievenue, Lisa, *Teach Yourself Decision-Aiding Software,* (University Press of America, 1992), 318 pages.
6. Nagel, Long, John, and Mills, Miriam, *Evaluation Analysis with Microcomputers,* (JAI Press, 1989), 474 pages.
7. Saaty, Thomas, *Decision-Making for Leaders: The Analytical Process for Decisions in a Complex World,* (Wadsworth, 1982).

8. Snellen, Ignace, Wim Van De Donk, and Jean-Paul Baquaist (eds.), *Expert Systems in Public Administration: Evolving Practices and Norms,* (Elsevier, 1989), 334 pages.
9. Thierauf, Robert, *Creative Computer Software for Strategic Thinking and DecisionMaking: A Guide for Senior Management and MIS Professionals,* (Quorum Books, 1993), 340 pages.

V. OBTAINING THE SOFTWARE

A copy of the software can be obtained with extensive documentation for only $50 from Decision Aids, Inc., 711 Ashton Lane South, Champaign, IL 61820. The $50 covers both the software and a book entitled *Teach Yourself Decision-Aiding Software,* as well as a hotline service for using the software.

Chapter 4

HOW TO ENCOURAGE
ACADEMIC CREATIVITY

I. BASIC POINTS

1. Require all faculty members to submit an annual report indicating (1) articles written or book chapters written for edited books, (2) books authored, (3) books edited, (4) consulting activities for governments, corporations, or other entities that use academic knowledge, (5) papers presented or speeches made, (6) mentoring of Ph.D. or M.A. theses, (7) favorable book reviews or other reviews, (8) awards received, (9) grants received, (10) software developed, and (11) academic leadership roles.

2. A second way to encourage academic creativity is to see to it that merit raises bear some correlation to the data that is included in those annual reports. Each department head should be required to show a kind of regression, correlation, or simple graphic analysis showing the relations.

3. Have good facilities on campus in terms of library facilities, computer facilities, Internet, and secretarial. Make them all available without charge.

4. Grant money for travel for hiring research assistants.

5. Encourage the hiring of colleagues that work well together in stimulating each other. Show a preference for those who do co-authoring or co-editing.

6. Encourage good graduate students to work with faculty members on joining projects. Require seminar papers to be publishable either jointly or separately.

7. Submit articles on creative achievements to the departmental newsletters, the faculty newspaper, and professional newsletters like *PS* in Political Science.

8. Have weekly seminars in which faculty members present their ongoing research for about 1/2 an hour and the second 1/2 hour is spent in

questions and discussion. This should include both junior and senior faculty. Both attendance and participation should be expected.

9. Meetings at least partly devoted on how to make the department more productive and more creative. Creativity refers to innovative usefulness or useful innovation. It is a qualitative concept. Productivity is an important quantitative concept referring to how many books and articles are generated.

10. Creative teaching should also be encouraged. Reports should ask about new courses or new ways of teaching old courses.

11. Encourage faculty members to present their creative ideas in the classroom when appropriate and encourage obtaining feedback from both undergraduate and graduate students.

II. Broader Points

1. The above points can cover any field of knowledge including natural science, social science, and humanities. Chemists may need chemistry laboratories to facilitate creativity, whereas sculptors may need garages where they can make noise chiseling. Those separate ideas are sub-parts of the above ideas such as the idea to provide good facilities.

2. Virtually all of these points are highly applicable at the departmental level, the LAS or college level, and the all-university level of universities. Sometimes individual departments seek to encourage creativity but get little encouragement from the administration. Other times, departments emphasize crony awards rather than merit-treatment awards. In such cases the administration may provide no discouragement possibly because cronyism may be heavily part of the reward system at the college level and the all-university level.

3. These creativity ideas are applicable to both large universities and small colleges. All institutions of higher learning try to encourage creativity on the part of faculty and students. At least they should try to encourage creativity. That may be the most important skill or characteristic that students can acquire to enable them to be successful in life. Creativity should be encouraged on the part of faculty, partly so they can be good role models, for their students but also because their creativity can lead to improving the general quality of life. Bigger universities may have more money for facilities, but all universities and colleges should ask professors and departments to prepare annual reports that are distributed among the faculty within each department and in summary form across the department. Those reports should include publishing, teaching, and service activities, many of which may involve creativity as mentioned or implied in the first point above. Doing such reports costs very little and can send an important message that creativity and productivity are

desired. They thus have a high benefit/cost ratio in all universities and colleges that rightfully seek to encourage creativity and productivity rather than administrative cronyism.

4.   Departments, colleges, universities, and the general public need to recognize what may be referred to as the Babe Ruth Syndrome of creativity. Babe Ruth has lost to Hank Aaron as the lifetime home run king and to both Mark McGwire and Sammy Sosa as the season home run king. Babe Ruth, however, will probably never lose the title of lifetime strikeout king. He is way ahead of the field. It takes many strikeouts to hit a lot of home runs because swinging for the bleachers frequently means missing the ball completely. Likewise, universities and the general public need to accept that a lot of professors will waste their time striking out on as many as one hundred projects for every one project that turns out to be highly creative and useful. It is said that even at major universities, only five percent of the faculty write 95% of the books, but the overwhelming majority has tenure.

5.   Tenure is important for encouraging creativity. Without it, faculty members might tend to be much more cautious and conservative. That does not mean being conservative ideologically.   Universities tend a bit toward the left, especially in social sciences and humanities. The people who teach at universities, though, tend to be on a lifetime ego trip. They were fawned over as children, as students, and now by the students they teach. The 95% who are not heavy book producers may consciously or subconsciously resent the five percent who are. As a result, in times of scarce resources the majority might seek to lessen the resources that go to the more creative faculty. The justification might be an equalitarian one. It could be based on subjective criteria that relate to teaching or the quality of what is published. The important thing is that creative non-tenured faculty may not get tenure under such circumstances, and tenured faculty may find themselves pushed out by unpleasantness.   This may especially occur now that there is no compulsory retirement, and some of the most creative, productive faculty do not want to retire. Having tenure enables one to withstand that kind lose-lose jealousy especially if one is untenured or past the age for being bribed or threatened into early retirement.

Chapter 5

EQUALITY, EQUAL OPPORTUNITY, AND MERIT TREATMENT

All people are not created equal, but they should be given equal opportunity to be creative. Doing that, however, might require equalizing people genetically and in terms of childhood socialization. They can then have more equal opportunities. Maybe the correct concept is equal treatment under law as expressed by the U.S. Constitution and the U.S. Supreme Court.

Perhaps what is really important is merit treatment, with a floor below which no one is allowed to fall. Merit treatment means that inequalities above that floor are based as much as possible on one's interests, abilities, motivation, prior output, future potential, and other merit considerations. In this context, merit treatment means relevant to job performance. Thus in an ideal society, pay and other rewards would be based on such merit considerations, as much as possible.

Merit rewards encourage creativity. It is difficult to be creative if one is not rewarded for being creative. On the other hand, some argue that some discrimination encourages creativity to offset the discrimination. Such an argument might apply to moderate economic discrimination. That means not everyone has the same income or wealth. Moderate differentials can be an incentive to both the poor and the rich to get richer so long as the poor (especially children) are never allowed to fall below a minimum level on health, education, and necessities broadly defined. Even non-merit discrimination based on gender or ethnic affiliation is more demoralizing than inspirational.

Regardless of the pragmatic effects of merit treatment, it can be considered desirable as good in itself or in accordance with the golden rule of virtually all religions and ethical systems. The golden rule says, "Do unto others as you would have other do unto you." This emphasizes interaction between individuals. Merit treatment tends to emphasize interaction between ethnic groups, genders, and other demographic groups.

Merit treatment can also be extended to interaction among nations, which is the basis of free trade and the theory of comparative advantage. One can even say that the only major point on which Adam Smith and Karl Marx agreed is the basic principle of specialization and division of labor. That principle says people, groups, and nations should be encouraged to do whatever they can do best in terms of their abilities and interests for which there is a demand.

That makes merit treatment a high-level win-win principle. It is on e level along with the win-win importance of economic competition, lifetime education, new technologies, democracy, and peaceful dispute resolution.

Postscript: The editors of the *DEV*, *PE* and *C+* journals were unsure as to which of the three journals would be most appropriate for this filler item on merit treatment.

1. The item is relevant to *Developmental Policy Studies*, which is concerned with inequality between industrial countries and developing countries. Merit treatment is also essential or highly helpful to national economic development.
2. The item is also relevant to *Policy Evaluation* because a key policy problem in any country is how to deal with the privileges of the rich versus the deprivations of the poor, and how to facilitate people operating at their best.
3. The item is further relevant to *Creativity Plus* because discrimination discourages creativity, and merit treatment encourages it, especially along gender, ethnic, class, and other lines.

Chapter 6

THE ROLE OF LUCK IN CREATIVITY

Some cynics, skeptics, and sour-grapes people emphasize luck in being an inventor or a Nobel Prize winner. That may be highly questionable as compared to the role of skill in being a successful inventor or even a Nobel Prize winner.

Luck can be defined as good things happening to someone for which they are not responsible in any way. Luck usually means good luck. Bad luck is the absence of good luck or worse. Skill can be defined as good things happening to someone as a result of doing things to make them happen. We should not think of luck and skill as being dichotomous opposites. They should be thought of as points on a continuum. Thus good things happening might be 40% luck and 60% skill in a given situation. The point of this short article is that great inventions and Nobel Prize winning are close to 0% luck and 100% skill.

That is not true of all good things. If a person wins a lottery , that is usually close to 100% luck and 0% skill, especially if they buy only one of millions of tickets. Here, however, we are talking about great inventions and Nobel Prizes, not winning a lottery.

Thomas Edison is considered by many people to be one of the greatest inventors of all time. He never won a Nobel Prize because he was not in theoretical physics but rather into applying physics principles to numerous inventions, especially relating to light, sound, and electricity. He, however, is an example of miserable luck and great skill and perseverance. He tried over 700 filaments before he found one that could work in a meaningful light bulb. The filament had to be capable of carrying an electric current and thereby generating light for a substantially long time. The filament could not be too expensive to make or to use. It could not generate too much heat or be dangerous. After 700 tries, he arrived at a tungsten filament. If he had some luck he would have hit on tungsten the first try or the first 100, or at least the first 500. He had the skill to know that there were hundreds of possible filaments to try and the perseverance to do so.

Most inventions require lots of skill and perseverance. An example of an important invention that is frequently referred to as pure luck is the invention of penicillin. Alexander Fleming supposedly was about to eat a piece of bread. He observed mold on it. He hypothesized that the mold was killing some bacteria. He performed further experiments and found his hypothesis was correct. Penicillin was thus invented in the 1920s, although it did not get much use until World War II and after. He had the skill as a biochemist to suspect that mold might be an antibiotic. He had the skill to know how to test that suspicion. That is skill and not luck. Other related examples are much more skillful knowledge than luck such as Newton's alleged observing of an apple falling from a tree. Lots of people observe moldy bread before Alexander Fleming and they did not invent penicillin. Likewise, lots of people observed falling apples before Isaac Newton, and they did not invent Newtonian physics.

Not only is skill much more important than luck in great inventions, it is also highly important to believe in that principle even to the point of exaggerating the importance of skill. The reason is that by definition we have no control over luck. We do have a lot of control over developing our skills, knowledge, and perseverance. That does not mean we should be untruthful about the importance of skill versus luck. It means that when in doubt in trying to invent or be creative, it is much better to err in the direction of emphasizing skill rather than luck, chance, fate, or happenstance.

This does not mean that we should reject prayer and the supernatural. If praying to God for the skill and insight to solve a problem causes one to have more positive attitude toward finding a solution then that is fine. Whatever causes a more positive attitude toward using one's skills is probably good. Relying on prayer to the neglect of one's own skills is not so good. All religions believe in free will rather than the idea that people are puppets of God in a totally predetermined way. Such thinking implies that God wants people to solve their own problems using their own possibly God-given skills, rather than have God solve their problems for them. It should also be noted as quoted by Einstein that God does not run the universe as if it were a game of chance, rather a universe of internally consistent logic that is waiting to be discovered by skillful scientists who sometimes win Nobel Prizes for their skillful discoveries.

In ending this article, I could say good luck to all of you. Doing so would be completely contrary to the theme of the article. Instead I should say, "May you all be skillful in making good things happen including being usefully creative, especially with regard to developing better public policies for promoting worldwide peace, prosperity, and democracy."

PART TWO:

EXAMPLES OF CREATIVITY

Chapter 7

CREATIVE PEOPLE IN THE
SECOND AND THIRD MILLENNIA

Creativity Plus likes to talk about causes and effects of creativity. It also likes to talk about examples of creativity and creative people. Two recent publications attempt to list the 100 most creative people for the second millennium of 1000-2000 and the third millennium of 2000-3000.

I. THE SECOND MILLENNIUM 1000-2000

The publication for the second millennium is entitled *Biography of the Millennium: 100 People, 1000 Years.* It is from a survey of experts by the A&E Television Networks. It may overemphasize the last 100 years and creative Americans, but it still seems quite appropriate and interesting. The tapes can be obtained from the A&E World, 19 Gregory Drive, South Burlington, VT 05403.

The creative people are not grouped, but one can group them into such categories as (1) scientists and inventors from natural and social science, (2) artists from music, literature, and visual arts, (3) political and military figures from all over the world, and (4) miscellaneous creative people.

What they all have in common is being highly creative in their respective fields with substantial impact on subsequent human activity. Some of these creative people were evil such as Hitler and Stalin. They may, however, not meet the definition of creativity since creativity is defined as being usefully innovative, and evil is the opposite of useful. The A&E people do not refer to the list of 100 people as being creative. The people are referred to as being "greatest," most admired," unforgettable personalities," "profoundly significant," and "changed our world in ways beyond imagining." all in one descriptive paragraph.

The top 20 people in rank order are:

1. Johann Gutenberg c1400-1468. Inventor of printing press.

2. Isaac Newton 1642-1727. Master of mathematics, physics, scientific revolution.
3. Martin Luther 1383-1546.   Leader Protestant Revolution. Faith for salvation.
4. Charles Darwin 1809-1882. Theory of Evolution.
5. William Shakespeare 1564-1616. World's most famous writer.
6. Christopher Columbus 1451-1506.   Spread culture of Europe to America.
7. Karl Marx 1818-1883. Evil capitalism. Working class would rise from oppression.
8. Albert Einstein 1879-1955. Theory of Relativity, Worked for peace.
9. Nicolaus Copernicus 1479-1543. Understanding of solar system.
10. Galileo 1564-1642. Science of modern astronomy.
11. Leonardo Da Vinci 1452-1519. Renaissance man.
12. Sigmund Freud 1856-1939. Exploration of the mind and psychotherapy.
13. Louis Pasteur 1822-1895. Pasteurization and vaccine for rabies.
14. Thomas Edison 1847-1931. Great inventor, e.g., electric light, motion pictures.
15. Thomas Jefferson 1743-1826. Declaration of Independence and Bill of Rights.
16. Adolf Hitler 1889-1945. Overthrow of Europe, Nazism, Holocaust.
17. Mahatma Gandhi 1869-1948. Non-violent civil disobedience.
18. John Locke 1632-1704. Life, liberty, property, and pursuit of happiness.
19. Michelangelo 1475-1564. Renaissance art, e.g., St. Peter's Cathedral.
20. Adam Smith 1723-1790. Economic theory of free trade and capitalism.

II. THE THIRD MILLENNIUM 2000-3000

The counterpart publication for the third millennium is entitled *A View from the Year 3000: A Ranking of the 100 Most Influential Persons at the End of the Year 2999.* It is authored by Arturo Kukeni which is the pseudonym for Michael Hart. The book is published by Poseidon Press. This list especially emphasizes people who invent solutions to 1999 problems, but who do so over the next thousand years.

Just as the A&E book emphasizes the 1900's, this book probably emphasizes the first 100 years of the third millennium. That is not because 2000-2100 is the most creative century of the third millennium. On the contrary, subsequent centuries are likely to be more creative in view of how new inventions are occurring at an exponential rate or a geometric progression. Each new invention tends to roughly generate two others. There may be a plateauing out for narrowly defined fields like the automobile, the airplane, the radio, and the television set, but there is new growth in their broader fields of transportation and communication. Technological and other change is also explosive if one combines the S-shaped curves for all the narrowly defined fields before they plateau out.

The reason for the emphasis on the first century of the third millennium is because the likely happenings after 2100 are probably beyond our present comprehension. People in the year 1000 probably could not comprehend what has happened in the 1900's or any 100 years subsequent to the Renaissance or the Industrial Revolution.

To make the futurist list shorter and more useful, we have eliminated the names of people, their birthdates, and when they died. Instead, each person is designated as X1, X2, X3, and so on. Ten of the 100 creative people from 2000-3000 are listed below. They were chosen by Michael Marien, the editor of the *Future Survey* in reviewing the Kukeni book in the October issue of the *Future Survey*.

X1. The most influential person in history who brought us immortality by growing new brain tissue in vitro and uploading all memory and personality into computers.

X2. Who devised a method of downloading information into the human brain so as to achieve desired personality changes.

X3. Who led a rebellion against a would-be global dictator.

X4. Who devised a set of safe, quick, and completely reversible techniques for sex-change.

X11. Primarily responsible for designing the constitutional system of the world government.

X22. Inventor of the first practical system for generating cheap power by nuclear fusion.

X23. The leading artistic figure of all time, who wrote and produced holovision plays.

X26. Who was chiefly responsible for the first space colony.

X28. Most responsible for the planetary engineering of Mars into an exhilarating human habitat.

X31. Inventor of a vaccine that protects humans from cancer.

Other future notables are described who developed nano-technology, explained macro-economics in a world of abundance (where three-quarters of the population is retired), wrote the greatest novels, invented personal robots, unified the Arab states into a durable entity, devised practical techniques for cleaning up ocean pollution, became the greatest cook of all time, developed the first usable system for psychokinesis, became the greatest poet ever, developed cryonics for restoring frozen human bodies to health, and captained the first successful interstellar expedition.

Chapter 8

SOCIETAL INVENTIONS

The concept of invention over-emphasizes technology and thus comes to the conclusion that the world's greatest inventions include the printing press, the telephone, the electric light, the steam engine, the automobile, and the computer. Much more important or at least equally important are social inventions in economics, social interaction, political organization, and in the humanities, including philosophy, language, and the arts.

The sum total of all those invention may be worth more than inventing the telephone also worth more than the telephone plus the light bulb. One, however, does not have to choose between Checkers and the light bulb. The important point is that these kind of social inventions tend to get ignored when one talks about inventions. They are inventions. They are not discoveries. Nobody discovered Checkers out there in the wilderness.

What this adds up to is a lot of societal inventions with regard to economic, social, and political institutions. The concept of inventions has been overly confined to can openers, mouse traps, safety pins, etc. As contrasted to really big inventions like (1) money system rather than barter, (2) democracy rather than some alpha gorilla leading a tribe, or (3) the invention of the United Nations as a way of bringing peace among countries.

I. ECONOMIC

Economic organization has to do with the buying and selling of goods. That definitely goes beyond animals that have never been known to operate a Wal-Mart or even a mom and pop grocery store.

Forms of business such as sole proprietorship, partnership, corporation, cooperative.

Ways of *raising capital* including through taxes, banks taking in savings accounts, selling stocks and bonds on the stock market, capital that comes from the sales of goods, and capital that comes from selling off assets.

There are ways of *paying for labor* such as by the hour, by how much is actually done which is determined after the job is over, also a flat rate before the job is started. Also contingency fees where one gets nothing unless the job meets a minimum specification.

Economic inventions include the international economic community and other kinds of *working together* such as mergers, conspiracies, alliances, unions, trade associations, and free trade zones.

Different ways of *organizing labor*. One way is each person makes a whole product, or each team makes a whole product. Another way is each person or team only makes part of a product, and then the parts are assembled further down on an assembly line. Workers could work by hand, with simple machines, or with computerized machines. That is getting into technology though, rather than economic organization.

Land ownership is a human invention, including joint tenancy, tenancy in common, fee simple, ownership with contracting out. The person on the other side of the contract may be a tenant farmer, a sharecropper, or a farm worker.

Economic organization also relates to how to organize the total economy which gets into concepts like socialism, capitalism, feudalism, fascism, communism.

Different kinds of *taxes* like income, sales, property, luxury and sin taxes on liquor, playing cards, and tobacco.

Inventions for fighting inflation and unemployment such as the Federal Reserve System, Keynesian economics, and economic growth ideas.

II. SOCIAL

Social organization mainly relates to how different groups are supposed to relate to each other including ethnic groups, racial groups, and religious groups. Past social organization has been discriminatory. Present social organization emphasizes merit *treatment*, which is a pretty important invention.

Human beings have invented *religions* including the five major religions of the world of Judaism, Christianity, Islam, Hinduism, and Buddhism. Animals do not have religion, although some people say they have souls or at least that household pets do, but maybe only the nice ones. Maybe poodles do, but not pit bulls.

Inventing the *family* or at least the traditional family with a division of labor between the father, mother, husband, wife, eldest son, eldest daughter, grandparents, and grandchildren. The exact division of labor varies from culture to culture, but there are underlying similarities. One might argue that those similarities are genetic, and that they are not an invention. Animals have families, and we generally do not think of animals as being inventors.

Humans have invented ways of training, *educating*, and socializing, meaning preschools, elementary schools, high schools, colleges, adult education, and on-the-job training.

III. POLITICAL

Animals have *governments* in the sense of an alpha gorilla that is the king in the gorilla group who gets there by physical force, rather than election. Human beings have invented elections. It is rather difficult to say that humans are genetically programmed to have elections, campaign contributions, and billboards.

Humans invented *legal* systems including the Babylonian legal system, the Judaic legal system as expressed in the five books of Moses, the Roman legal system, the medieval Canon Law system, the Napoleonic Code, the Anglo American common law, and the contemporary American statute law. Constitutional law is more tied in with government. Legal systems also include the judicial process for determining what the law means and especially for applying law to specific cases.

Humans have invented *international* systems which include the United Nations, economic communities like NAFTA, European Community, GAT, military alliances like NATO or the Allies, the axis powers, and international organizations like World Health and International Postal.

IV. HUMANITIES

Humans have invented *philosophical systems* such as empiricism versus rationalism, materialism versus supernaturalism, socialism versus capitalism, utilitarianism versus art for art's sake, with more specific schools and sub-schools of philosophy just like there are lots more specific religions and sub-religions.

Humans have also invented *art forms* including painting, literature, sculpture, and music.

Humans have invented leisure-type activities including *sports* like basketball, football, baseball, Parcheesi, tiddlywinks, monopoly, fish, and Old Maid.

Chapter 9

ARTISTIC CREATIVITY

The purpose of this article is to discuss artistic creativity. Previous related articles have discussed policy creativity such as "Creative Legislation" in Autumn, 2000 *Creativity Plus*. Subsequent articles will discuss business creativity and academic scientific creativity.

Artistic creativity can be defined as developing widely-acclaimed beauty in music, literature, or the visual arts of painting, sculpture and architecture. This article is organized in terms of (1) the usefulness of art since creativity is innovative usefulness or useful innovation, (2) subjectivity-bias including class, market, ethnic, and gender bias, (3) cultural relativity, including both relativity and objectivity examples, (4) expanding artistic creativity to include all five senses, (5) the use of computers in artistic creativity, (6) the role of genes, (7) creativity in performing rather than composing, (8) inspirational art, and (9) policy implications.

I. USEFULNESS

The usefulness of art is somewhat questionable. The best that can maybe be said for it is that it entertains people. They get some pleasure out of looking at paintings, listening to music, reading books.

We are here talking about pure art, not books that are textbooks to educate. Pure art refers to books that are "well-written" fiction to entertain. We are not talking about pictures that are diagrams of the inside of a computer. That would be functional art.

We are also not talking about art for inspiration which could include (1) pictures of heroes, (2) music that is folk music, and (3) books and poetry that are inspirational. We are talking about music that has pure sounds and no program, including the music of Bach or Beethoven, rather than music that might inspire a football team or an army. We are talking about the paintings of Rembrandt, rather than Norman Rockwell on freedom of speech, freedom from fear, and freedom from want. For arty people, those Rockwell paintings are some kind of cornball folk art, like folk music.

II. Subjectivity and Bias

A. Class-Biased Subjectivity

If we are talking about visual art, audio art, and reading art as pure art, then we may also be talking about something that is partly phony in terms of the people who claim that it has some kind of value. Their motivation is often a form of elitist snobbism. This is easily proved by showing an elitist a picture and saying that it is a Hyman Schwartz painting. In reality, the alleged Van Gogh may have been painted by Hyman Schwartz and the alleged Hyman Schwartz picture may have been a Van Gogh. To elitist snobs, the picture means almost nothing. It is just a matter of who the painters are and what the other elitist snobs say about them.

Likewise, one could do a test case in which Irving Berlin (substitutes for Norman Rockwell) and Beethoven (for Rembrandt). We need to find something by Irving Berlin that sounds classical enough to fool a snob. We could also find a short excerpt from a Beethoven symphony that sounds like popular music. It is easy to find a piece of Shakespeare maybe or Dickens that sounds like popular writing, and find something by Norman Mailer that sounds like it was written a hundred years ago. Being old and noncontemporary seems to especially appeal to elitist snobs.

There is a kind of political and economic conservatism in fancy art. It is an expensive habit that the poor cannot afford when we are talking about (1) Rembrandts, rather than girlie pictures, and (2) going to the opera rather than playing a harmonica or a fiddle. One can argue that it is more difficult (1) to paint a Rembrandt than to do a girlie photograph, and more difficult (2) to compose or perform an opera than to do likewise for a harmonica or fiddle. Difficulty, however, is not beauty. Otherwise, a perfect counterfeit dollar which is difficult to make would be considered beautiful, which it is not. Likewise, a Kodak snapshot of great scenery which is easy to photograph would not be considered beauty, which it is.

B. Market- or Price-Biased

One could also argue that a Rembrandt sells for a lot more than an issue of Playboy, and a ticket to an opera sells for a lot more than a ticket to a fiddle concert. Price is determined partly by supply, and there is a small supply of Rembrandt painters and opera composers. Price is also determined partly by demand, which is desire plus ability to pay. Rembrandt buyers and opera-ticket buyers do have a lot more ability to pay. Nevertheless, price does not equal beauty. Otherwise, a billion dollar B-1 bomber would be considered a thing of beauty, rather than at best a necessary evil of the ugliness of war. Likewise, a newborn baby is generally considered beautiful, but they usually cost virtually nothing to have throughout the world.

Libertarian and free-market conservatives would like to think that the marketplace somehow determines beauty or at least worthwhile art. Most people would say this is obviously not always so. A KISS rock concert can bring in a lot more money than either a Jascha Heifetz violin concert or a Woodie Gurthrie guitar concert. Most people, however, would question whether the rock concert is more beautiful. If conservatives and liberals differ on Heifetz versus Guthrie, then this shows that beauty may be ideologically biased or class biased.

C. Ethnic- and Gender-Biased

The subjectivity and elitism of music, painting, and literature may be shown by the fact that women and members of minority groups, like Jews, were not considered good composers, painters, or authors until the twentieth century. The explanation is partly that the critics who determined good art from the Renaissance to the twentieth century may have been biased against women and Jews. This may be especially true in painting where the subjectivity is greater than it is in composing music or writing novels. The greater subjectivity in painting allows prejudice to enter more easily.

The ability of women, Jews, and blacks to paint, compose music, or write literature probably did not greatly improve over the last half of the twentieth century. Their abilities were, however, more recognized by critics who were less likely to be as biased as previously. There was also a lack of opportunities to get into painting, music, and literature. Women, Jews, and blacks also had fewer opportunities to get into medicine, law, business, and college teaching than males, non-Jews, and whites. Nevertheless, they succeeded more in those fields where merit treatment is more objective. Note that in the early 1900s, Jews succeeded as performers on the piano and on the violin and as popular composers. Objectivity is greater there than in what constitutes "great" music composing or "great" art.

III. Cultural Relativity

A. Relativity Examples

Artistic beauty and creativity are also highly culturally relative, as well as class, market, ethnic, and gender biased. Poor people in Russia, for example, sincerely love ballet when ballet may be a form of conspicuous consumption for people in the United States. Likewise, poor people in Italy sincerely love opera, but opera may also be a vehicle for pretentious displays by the leisure class or its aspirants. Likewise, low--income Japanese people seem to enjoy formal poetry, including complicated Haiku poems.

More important, beauty is quite divergent across different cultures studied by anthropologists, archeologists and scholars of comparative music, painting, and literature. The older the art is the more admired and expensive it might be. Also, art made in exotic places may be relatively high priced, but not sandals or tee shirts.

B. Objectivity Examples

In spite of the diversity, there may be some underlying principles of artistic beauty that cut across time-periods, places, and also across the three basic art forms of painting, music and literature.   Specific examples of all three art forms can be positioned on a continuum. At one extreme on the continuum are reproductions of exact reality. At the opposite extreme are displeasing distortions of reality. In the middle are pleasing capturings of the essence of reality.

This general principle can be applied to painting, music, and literature. Paintings should not be mere photographs because taking a photograph is generally not an act of creativity, although inventing the camera is. At the other extreme, a painting should not distort reality in a way that most people would find unpleasant. It is acceptable to paint melting watches to illustrate slow-passing time like Salvador Dali, or to paint exploding body parts to illustrate the evils of the Spanish Civil War like Pablo Picasso. It is not artistically acceptable to do so-called mud painting anymore than it is artistically creative to take a photograph.

Likewise music should not be a mere tape recording of birds chirping, since turning on a tape recorder is not an act of creativity, although inventing a tape recorder is. At the other extreme, playing instruments randomly may constitute pure noise and thus be equally unacceptable as artistic creativity.   In the middle is impressionistic music that is generally pleasing and neither an exact reproduction of real world sounds, nor a grotesque distortion of concepts of rhythm, melody, harmony, lyrics, and other music components.

Literature may allow for more diversity than painting or music. Super-reality literature including a play could be a camcorder of people in a shopping market, a subway train, or some other everyday place for a few hours.   Camcording the dialogue, costuming, and sets is not an act of creativity, although inventing the camcorder is. At the opposite extreme would be some literature composed by an average set of monkeys, although theoretically if they hit enough computer keys, they may do a piece from Shakespeare.

Knowing there may be this kind of underlying artistic beauty and creativity, however, does not tell us much. It only tells us what good painting, music, and literature is not. It allows too much room in the middle for class, market, ethnic, gender, and cultural bias. That is both bad and good. It is possibly bad because It reflects adversely on the objectivity of artistic beauty. It is possibly good because it allows a lot of room for different strokes (brush, baton, and pen) for different folks, but that raises further issues of individual and group relativity.

On the objectivity of beauty, we are talking about art, as contrasted to biological or environmental beauty. Biological beauty among human beings and higher animals is probably closely associated with being healthy. Physical beauty in women and men correlates highly with being healthy and capable of reproducing healthy children. Beauty in the environment tends to mean conductive to healthy people.   Thus a polluted or impoverished environment is considered relatively ugly. A pollution-free sky or an expensively manicured suburb is considered relatively beautiful. However, with minor exceptions, only God can create a tree or a beautiful human being, and thus creating trees and people are not considered forms of human creativity.

IV. THE FIVE SENSES AND COMPUTERS

A. The Five Senses

Beauty is frequently said to be in the eye of the beholder, but it can be in the eye, ear, mind, nose, taste, or touch as well. Painting appears to the sense of sight. Much appeals to the sense of hearing. Literature appeals to the thinking aspects of the mind, including conjuring up the five senses. We do not have much concern for beauty with regard to smells, tastes, or feels. The art of cooking relates to both smelling and tasting. Touching may get into sexual love play.

Just as other forms of art are highly relative, but also have elements of objectivity, so do these art forms. Most of the world likes such foods as ice cream and cashew nuts, but much food is culturally relative such as caviar in Russia or whale meat in Japan. What tastes good is highly age relative, with children almost worldwide preferring hamburgers and french fries. Food serves a biological function that painting and music do not. Likewise, so does sexual touching.

In this context, we are concerned not so much with what constitutes beauty in smells, tastes, or touches, but what constitutes creativity. There is creativity in designing recipes, making perfumes and writing literature like the Kama Sutra which deals with sensuous touching. However, there does not seem to be anybody in the realm of smells, tasting, and touching comparable to Rembrandt, Beethoven, and Shakespeare.

B. Computers and Artistic Creativity

Trying to write a program for computerized music, poetry, or other art forms may provide useful insights into the components of music, poetry, or other art forms. Doing so, however, does not lessen the subjectivity. Doing so just moves it from the music composer to the computer programmer. It is challenging to create a virtual reality of sights, sounds, smells, tastes, and touches.

Doing so however, may not have much value as compared to the real thing. Receiving the taste of a turkey dinner through a caliper connected to a computer is no substitute for receiving a real turkey. When the time comes that we can transmit turkeys through computers, we will probably also be able to fax whole people to Paris without losing an arm in London the way.

Computers can aid in doing art although less creatively such as MacArt, PowerPoint, or animation. They can enable downloading of music, pictures, and eventually videotapes. They can aid in word processing, literature, keeping artistic records, or doing statistical art research.

V. GENETICS, INNOVATIVENESS, AND INSPIRATION

Artistic creativity is not something that is earned as much as business, science, or policy creativity. It is more likely to be born not made. People who can paint realistically or who can sing opera have a special genetically acquired talent. Literature is more an acquired skill. If the skill is something one is born with, it does not seem so appropriate to give the holder a lot of credit, at least not a lot of credit for creativity. A 400 pound football player who can run the 100 yard dash in 10 seconds probably did not work very hard to achieve that skill, but he may be worth millions to a football team owner. It is a bit inappropriate when the 400 pound fullback runs for a touchdown in 10 seconds covering the 100 yard field to have people say (1) how brilliant he is when it is possible he cannot even read and write, and (2) how creative he is when it is possible he has a hard time thinking out tic-tac-toe. Likewise, an opera singer or a great painter may simply have that part of his or her brain much better developed from birth than the average person. I do not think that Edison was genetically programmed to invent the light bulb, the phonograph, movie projector, or hearing aid.

Some pianists, violinists, and actors are considered highly creative when they are basically following a script that some truly creative person may have developed. When we talk about art, though, we are talking more about people who create art, not perform other people's creations, meaning (1) the composer of symphonies and not the band leader or the violinist, (2) the author of a play and not the parrot who mouths the words. It may take great skill to play a violin well or a piano. It also takes great skill to type fast. We definitely need people who have great skills. We especially need, for example, brain surgeons who can skillfully transplant brains or other surgeons who transplant hearts, kidneys, livers, and genitalia. That is not creativity, even though those are valuable skills. The person who invented the typewriter was creative. Likewise, the person who invented brain surgery, or who did the very first heart transplant was creative. Those who copy something that somebody created are not creators, even if it requires great skill and usefulness to do the copying.

Art can be important to inspire creativity, but that is not the kind of art that arty people say is good art. I especially like the statue I have of Thomas Jefferson because he symbolizes the Bill of Rights, the Declaration of Independence, free speech, separation of church and state, due process, the Constitution, and the Revolutionary War. I would not be especially bothered if I were to find out the statue came from a mold and was not even made by hand. The important thing is does it inspire? I would be more inspired by an appropriate reprint than an inappropriate original.

VI. POLICY IMPLICATIONS

This article discusses the nature of artistic creativity and thus indirectly the nature of beauty. This is journal of the Policy Studies Organization. We should therefore say something about artistic creativity, beauty, and public policy. We have mentioned that painting, music, and literature can inspire improvements in public policy.

Likewise, public policy can inspire artistic creativity in various ways such as:

1. Providing funding to innovative composers, artists, authors, and performers as is done by the National Endowment for the Humanities and the National Endowment for the Arts.
2. Providing funding for public schools and public parks where art, music, and literature lessons and appreciation are provided, thereby encouraging participation rather than merely being a spectator.
3. Taxpayer-supported art institutes, concert halls, and public broadcasting may be justified as entertaining and even inspiring, but they are not as relevant to encouraging artistic creativity as policies 1 and 2.

VII. SOME CONCLUSIONS

In light of that, we might say the value of art is a wash in the sense that some of it is used by snobs to make other people feel inferior or to try to do so. But other art makes people feel good and inspired.

We are, however, somewhat off the subject of artistic creativity when we talk about good and bad art, as contrasted to creative and uncreative. The bottom line is that creativity has two key elements. One is new and innovative. The second is being socially useful. Something that is merely new and innovative but useless may be innovative, but not creativity. Likewise, something that is highly useful, such as a stapler, was only creative when it was first invented. Thus "art" can be (1) innovative but not useful, (2) useful but not innovative, (3) neither useful nor innovative, or (4) both useful and innovative. The last category may be the kind of art that is worth striving for.

Chapter 10

BUSINESS CREATIVITY

I. MEASUREMENT

People judge technological creativity by how many patents one has taken out. That is a poor criterion. One patent for the light bulb may be worth 100 patents on trivial variations of a belly button lint picker. To determine the quality of a new technology, we look to see its impact in creating new industries, new employment, and new income.

Likewise, business creativity may not have much to do with how much income one earns. A CEO may earn 400K a year but that CEO was chosen by the Board of Directors of General Motors or some well established corporation to run the place. That is not business creativity.

One would not want to go so far as to say that anybody on salary rather than commission or percentage of the profits is not creative. Mr. Iacocca received a salary from Chrysler that was considered creative in getting a failing company to become profitable. He was paid probably more than salary. He probably got a percentage of the profits.

Maybe the most creative kind of business creativity involves starting a business from scratch like Bill Gates and Microsoft and working it into being highly successful in terms of gross income, net profit, quantity of employees, quantity of customers, industries that are suppliers, industries that are buyers.

II. START-UPS

It is hard to be creative or very creative in traditional existing business such as a grocery store, or a drug store, a dry cleaners. Small businesses do frequently expand. They expand by opening branches and franchises. A single Kroger grocery store may become a hundred of them. The other 99 may not be that different than the first one. All 100 may not be that different than thousands of super markets. There has to be a big chunk of innovation in order to be creative, not merely a big chunk. Amazon.com creatively established a new way to market books and lots of other products. Mr. Kroger did not invent the grocery store business.

It is probably more conducive to creativity to be in a business that one owns rather than one works for, all other things held constant. It is likewise more conducive to creativity to be in a business that is relatively new in the economic or business history of the world than to be in a rather traditional business where one makes small incremental changes on how things are traditionally done.

Examples of exciting new business often go with exciting new technologies. Alexander Graham Bell to some extent began the business of the telephone company. Thomas Edison began the business of the electric light company. They did not merely invent the telephone and the electric light, respectively. They were also business people. Bill Gates supposedly never invented DOS or Windows 95. He hired programmers to develop ideas that they had already started or somebody else had already started. He is primarily a business person, not an inventor. Steve Jobs from Apple seems to have done more with regard to inventing pull down menus, click on icons, split screens, drag and drop, and other user friendly operating system options. Windows 95 copied them and required no dedicated hardware to use them as Apple did.

III. INCENTIVES AND FACILITATORS

The profit motive is important in business creativity. It may not be so important in technological creativity. Lots of new technologies are developed by academics in universities who are motivated to develop new knowledge for the fun of it or the prestige. The profit motive though can cause a business person to be willing to work maybe 18 hours a day, seven days a week, to build up a business. Idealistic academics can also work 18 hours a day, 7 days a week, but on developing new knowledge, not on building up a business.

I am not sure that getting a masters degree in business has much to do with business creativity. Although I am not sure that getting a masters degree or a PhD degree in anything has much to do with creativity. The reason for saying that is that there are lots of people with graduate degrees who are not necessarily very creative in terms of inventing anything or developing new knowledge. A better way to put it is that a PhD degree does not guarantee creativity in whatever field the PhD is in. However, if one wants to be a highly creative physicist, one had better learn what has already been done and why, so one can reason by analogy to new physics ideas. Likewise with biology, music, psychology, and other fields. That is also true of business. An MBA does not guarantee that one will be creative in business. However if one wants to be highly creative in modern business, it is definitely helpful to know what has been previously developed regarding business principles of production, marketing, labor-management relations, consumer relations, raising capital, location matters, and other business knowledge and skills.

IV. ETHNIC GROUPS

Certain ethnic groups have been associated with entrepreneurial activity during at least the first half of the 20th century. This includes Jews in Eastern Europe and in big cities in the U.S., although formerly rural peddlers and small town haberdashery merchants. It also includes Hindus and Pakistanis in East Africa from Kenya to South Africa. It includes the Chinese of Southeast Asia from the Philippines to Thailand where they are sometimes referred to as the Jews of the Orient.

The explanations in the case of the Jews are that they were not allowed to own land, and they were reluctant to do so since one cannot carry one's land on one's back when the next expulsion occurs. They also were allowed to be money lenders when it was considered un-Christian before the Protestant Reformation.

Ambitious immigrants tended to go into retailing in order to save money by doing one's own labor, so they could send their children to college and professional schools. Immigrants logically tend to be ambitious people from over-populated countries like China and India, or who are severely discriminated against like the Jews of East Europe or the Irish of the British Empire before Irish independence. The Irish tended to be more rural and less commercial than the Jews. They were more likely to drift into factories having a lack of capital for becoming a farm owner. The Jews have now been replaced in American retailing by Koreans, Arabs, Southeast Asians, and Wal-Mart.

One explanation for why the Chinese tend to be retailers and the Japanese tend to be manufacturers is that China has always allowed landowners to will away their land to all their children, but Japan has traditionally only allowed the first son to inherit. This results in small farm plots in China and big landed estates in Japan. This also results in Chinese immigrants to Hawaii being especially oriented toward small retail shops, and Japanese immigrants to Hawaii being oriented toward manufacturing and other bigger establishments.

As of the year 2000, business creativity refers to start-up companies that relate to the Internet, electronic business, computer software, or computer hardware. On an international level, some key cities include in alphabetical order Bangalore India, Tel-Aviv Israel, Silicon Valley California, and possibly Beijing China. The Silicon Valley represents a variety of ethnic groups including non-ethnic Americans, along with East Indians, Chinese (and other Asians), and Jews with technical rather than business

The ethnic Indians, Chinese, and Jews may have in common a cultural affinity for manipulating numbers and words that may be associated with some aspects of Hinduism, Judaism, and Confucianism. The Indians did invent Sanskrit and Indo-European languages. The Jews and their Phoenician and Arabic relatives did invent the alphabet and the Arabic numbering system. The Chinese invented the abacus and the only major surviving pictograph language and numbering system (like the Romans) does not use position to indicate tens or twelves.

Chapter 11

CREATIVE BUDGETING

A. SOME CREATIVE BUDGETING IDEAS

1.   The Policy Studies Organization may not want its revenues to greatly exceed its expenses, because this may indicate a lack of creativity in thinking of ways to spend our income.

2.   For the same reasons, we may not ant our assets to greatly exceed our liabilities.

3.   We are not a not-for-profit corporation. We pay no dividends to shareholders and thus do not have this pressure.

4.   We do not want to waste money. Thus, we will buy X units for Y dollars where $Y is the lowest price available, holding constant information and transaction costs.

5.   Our greatest expenses and liabilities are the immeasurable opportunity costs we suffer when we fall to develop effective and efficient ideas for promoting the application of political and social science to important policy problems.

6.   Our greatest income and assets are the immeasurable benefits we receive as a result of publishing articles, journals, book chapters, and books that have an impact on improving public policy.

7.   Those assets include the PSO members and others who write and edit those articles, journals, book chapters, and books.

8.   Policy studies may be the highest form of knowledge because it deals with how governmental activities can encourage better natural science, social science, and humanities.

9.   A high form of policy studies may be win-win policy studies because it deals with public policy that can enable all major sides in a public policy controversy to come out ahead of their best initial expectations simultaneously.

10. An even higher form of policy studies and knowledge in general may be the study of creativity since knowledge relevant to increasing creativity can help bring about improvements in public policy, business,

technology, social relations, democracy, international relations, law, the arts, and other fields of knowledge. Thus, money spent for trying to improve creativity may be well-spent, even if it does not succeed. Many non-successes may be needed for each substantial success for being usefully innovative in solving diverse problems.

B. CREATIVELY INCREASING EXPENSES TO REDUCE THE DEFICIT

We at PSO are sometimes asked, "How can small organizations afford five journals?" The key answer is that we cannot afford to have less than five journals.

"How is that?" The answer is that we used to have only one journal called the *Policy Studies Journal* and we had a terrible deficit of expenses exceeding income. This was partly because *PSJ* was the world's only quarterly that came out eight times a year. Such a situation can be resolved by either reducing expenses (and thus reducing services to members), or by increasing income (through increased services to members). Having the second quarterly journal of the *Policy Studies Review* did generate new members and new income, thereby temporarily wiping out the annual deficit.

Soon the deficit came back as the length of journals increased. We then added three more quarterly journals: *Policy Evaluation, Developmental Policy,* and *Creativity Plus.* By offering five quarterlies, we greatly increased the willingness of libraries to pay much higher subscription fees. This (for now) again wipes out the deficit. We anticipate, though, as a result of increasing our activities, the deficit will return. At that time, we will further increase our activities in order to be more attractive to individual members and libraries which will result in increased income and a reduced deficit.

One moral to this story is that we need more business in government, as Ronald Reagan said. By that he especially meant we need more practicing of the business principle that it takes a willingness to spend money to make money. Bill Clinton also said it takes a government that is willing to invest and thereby increase its expenses in new technology and training in order to (1) wipe out the national deficit, (2) create a surplus, and (3) double the gross national product.

Both presidents had similar win-win can-do philosophies. Reagan, however, believed that across-the-board tax increases would be automatically channeled into productive investment. Instead, it was channeled into real estate, luxury goods, and high CEO salaries. The wasted tax cut combined with the arms race more than doubled the national debt, as contrasted to more than doubling the national income.

David Stockman, Ronald Reagan's Director of the Office of Management and Budget, said the main purpose for government taxes was to provide earmarked tax breaks for activities that would improve productivity through new technologies and training. The secondary purpose was to raise revenue to support the government.

Unfortunately, Stockman's philosophy was considered contrary to a belief in the invisible hand of laissez faire, and he left the Reagan Administration.

The overall bottom line, when dealing with a small organization like PSO or a big organization like the USA, is when one has a deficit: (1) generally do not concentrate on decreasing expenses, (2) instead concentrate on developing new expenses that will bring in more income, (3) to not only wipe out the deficit, but also to fulfill the more positive functions of PSO and the USA.

Chapter 12

CREATIVITY AND HUMOR

I. WHAT IS BEING FUNNY?

We define creativity as being usefully innovative. Humor can be useful in uplifting people's spirits. That includes the jokester as well as the recipient. Although there may be Pagliacci exceptions. The best humor in terms of mutual or win-win uplift is interactive or even group humor so long as the group is small enough so as to allow everybody to participate. They should also be similar in subject matter interests or at least dovetailing in the sense of jokes about a priest, a Buddhist monk, and a rabbi on a football team.

Good humor should be creative in the innovative sense since most humor has rapid diminishing utility by virtue of depending on unanticipated punch lines and behavior. It is possible that a creativity test could be devised that relates to telling jokes. There once was a radio program called, "Can You Top This?" The panelists were given a subject matter that they had to convert into a funny joke. The laugh meter indicated how many points they received. They rotated the order in which they handled the subjects.

Joke telling illustrates that supposedly creative humor, like intelligence, may rely heavily on memory rather than spontaneous creativity. The winners on "Can You Top This" generally seemed to be the panelists who had the greatest store of jokes, possibly memorized from short or long encyclopedias arranged by subject matter. Likewise, what looks like intelligence may frequently involve having memorized problem solving techniques available in SAT, ACT, LSAT, and other IQ cram books.

Good joke telling may also involve a big element of acting ability. This was the case on "Can You Top This?" where the panelists would frequently do imitations of various ethnic groups, animals, and famous people. The laugh meter or applause meter may therefore not have been scoring creative humor so well. One might also note that the laugh provoking ethnic imitations of the 1950s might provoke severe scowls and withdrawing of radio-TV sponsors in the 1990s.

II. Place, Age, and Other Relativity

That's just one of many illustrations of the cultural relativity of humor. What is funny to children may not be funny to adults and vice versa. What is funny to lawyers may not appeal to other occupations. Likewise, humor differs across genders and especially across cultures and historic time periods. The jesters in medieval courts were frequently dwarfs who are more likely to be pitied or admired for their professional skills in contemporary times.

An underlying objectivity in creative humor is that it makes people laugh. That does not tell us much, since we want to know what is it in verbal or situational humor that makes people laugh. In both verbal and situational humor, the innovative element of surprise is important as mentioned above. There is, however, nothing especially funny about a surprise ending to a murder mystery in which the culprit is the narrator. It would be more funny if the culprit were the butler's talking horse. People find talking animals to be funny such as Mickey Mouse, Bugs Bunny, and Felix the Kat. Talking animals are unexpected, and they can get away with doing unexpected things. For a human being to behave like Mickey Mouse may be silly and for Mickey Mouse to behave too much like a human being would be boring.

Talking animals, however, are mainly funny to children or to rather youthful adults. Human comedians need to be slap stick to get children to laugh, but they need to be clever to get adults to laugh. Cleverness may relate to double or triple plays on words. It may relate to cleverness of teenagers in outwitting parents or vice versa. The concept of outwitting may bring a smile but not side splitting laughter, including spouses outwitting each other or business partners.

Side splitting laughter is difficult to generate among adults. When it happens, it frequently involves some kind of insider interaction that would not be funny to other people. Comedy in movies is designed to make a lot of people laugh, not just a few insiders. That kind of comedy may involve a combination of silly adult behavior but clever. Modern adults are not likely to laugh at feeble-minded people any more than they are to laugh at dwarfs as jesters. The silliness and cleverness may involve making fun of important political figures like President Clinton or presidential candidate Bush. The recipients of that kind of humor do not feel the humor is sadistic or bullying because the objects of the humor are considered big people who can take care of themselves and who will survive the jokes. The Supreme Court has held that public figures like Jerry Falwell are expected to be sufficiently hard-shelled to withstand even the humor of *Hustler* magazine in depicting Falwell having sex in an outhouse. Likewise, widely acceptable humor includes making fun of oneself as an acceptable form of self-abuse.

A key factor in generating big laughs is what might be called the contagion factor. That means if one is in a movie theater and everyone else is laughing, you laugh, otherwise you feel foolish. If, however, one is home alone watching the same movie on television then you might feel foolish if you laugh all by yourself. People may deliberately go to movie theaters to see funny movies with other people so as to benefit from that contagion factor. In that sense, humor can be a socializer in the sense of getting people to laugh together. Professor Putnam is worried that too many people are bowling alone. A more significant worry might be that there is a need for more funny movies where people can have a collective laugh. Other kinds of movies can be enjoyed alone more easily.

III. PURPOSES OF HUMOR

Purposes of humor (i.e., laugh-provoking statements, behavior, or situations) thus far mentioned include the following:

1. Relaxation, escape, uplift, and happy feelings
2. Poking fun at others in a way that may be more acceptable than explicit insults
3. Poking fun at oneself to show humility or to illustrate a point
4. To make money and/or be admired as a professional or amateur comedian
5. To generate sociable interaction in a group
6. To relieve boredom in a speech

Another purpose that humor serves is to enable people to talk about taboo subjects without being considered overly outrageous. This is especially the case with so-called dirty jokes. Perhaps they should be called sexual jokes so as to get away from the idea that sex is dirty. On the other hand, some dirty jokes are bathroom scatology. Even those jokes deserve some respectability. Only Americans call a toilet a bathroom or a washroom, as if bathing or washing was the main function of a toilet. Regardless of the euphemisms or the vulgarisms, sexual and scatological jokes generate laughs, sometimes even in mixed company possibly because they enable people to release pent-up feelings about sex and going to the bathroom-washroom-toilet.

IV. SOME CONCLUSIONS

From this rambling, we can possibly conclude the following about creativity and humor:

1. Humor is highly relative across time, places, genders, ethnic groups, and other ways of classifying people.
2. Humor relies on a clever element of surprise rather than cliches, but surprise that is not scary or overly cerebral.
3. Humor is especially age-related even more so than the other relativity characteristics mentioned in the above point. A new born baby may

smile in a humorous way in response to a smile, a tickle, or moving keys which may not affect an older child, let alone an adult.

4. Humor is useful for making people feel good, and when they feel good, they are more productive. One could, however, make a case for saying feeling good (like happiness) is an end in itself.

5. Joke telling is not so good as a test of creativity because it involves such a big element of memory and acting.

6. A humor-producer is one who tells jokes or does funny things that get big laughs. A humor-consumer is one who does lots of laughing, even at jokes that other people think are shallow or inane.

7. Laughter (like yawning and the mumps) is contagious. Unlike yawning and the mumps, however, laughing is good for the psyche and thus good for society, the polity, and the economy.

V. APPENDIX: HUMOR FROM PE, DEV, AND C+

To show that we practice what we preach about the desirability of humor, we will publish creative humor jokes that are sent to *Creativity Plus*, especially if they have public policy relevance. A good example is "The Poultry Farmer, The Nobel Prize, and the Pulitzer Prize" at page 8 of the Spring 2000 issue of *Creativity Plus*, or "A Bipartisan Impeachment Joke" at page 4 of the Spring 1999 Policy *Evaluation*. A better example might be the picture of the PSO editorial board at page 3 of the Spring 2000 *Policy Evaluation* or the picture entitled "One Pregnancy Per Person" showing a milk-bellied PSO workshop coordinator in China at page 10 of the Spring 1998 *Policy Evaluation*.

A. Policy Evaluation

1. "Some of the PSO editors" at page 3 of the Spring 2000 issue
2. "PSJ+PSR=31's" at page 33 of the Spring 2000 issue
3. "A Bipartisan Impeachment Joke" at page 4 of the Spring 1999 issue
4. "At the 1998 PSO-APSA Convention in Boston: at page 4 of the Winter 1998 issue of Policy *Evaluation*
5. "Sherman the Shark on Policy Evaluation" at page 10-11 of the Autumn 1998 issue of Policy *Evaluation*
6. "Dilbert on Win-Win Allocation" on page 4 of the Summer 1998 issue of Policy *Evaluation*
7. "One Pregnancy Per Person" on page 10 of the Spring 1998 issue of Policy *Evaluation*
8. "Mr. Boffo on Super-optimizing" on page 23 of the Spring 1998 issue of Policy *Evaluation*

9. 1997 PSO-APSA Meeting" at page 4 of the Winter 1997 issue of Policy *Evaluation*
10. "The Interdisciplinary Broadness of Policy Studies" at page 4 of the Autumn 1997 issue of Policy *Evaluation*
11. "Policy Research Infrastructure" at page 13 of the Autumn 1997 issue of Policy *Evaluation*
12. "PSO Members Voice Their Comments" at page 33 of the Autumn 1997 issue
13. "The PSO Baseball Team" at page 40 of the Autumn 1997 issue
14. "Two Policy Analysts on Vacation" at page 37 of the Autumn 1992 issue

B. Developmental Policy

1. "Participants in a PSO Policy Analysis Workshop in Thailand" at page 36 in the Autumn 2000 issue
2. "Is China Our Friend or Enemy" at page 7 of the Spring 2000 issue
3. "Please no Violence" at page 18 of the Spring 2000 issue
4. "PSO Work in China" at page 30 of the Summer 2000 issue
5. "U.S.-China Trade Talks" at page 15 of the Summer 1997 issue
6. "Who Knows Who Has the Bomb" at page 38 of the Summer 1997 issue

Chapter 13

ENCOURAGING CREATIVITY IN TECHNOLOGY, SCIENCE, AND GENERAL MATTERS

I. SOME POINTS REGARDING TECHNOLOGY CREATIVITY

More technology creativity can be encouraged especially dispersion if investors are guaranteed royalties rather than the exclusive right to manufacture. Bill Gates is a good example of that as contrasted to Steve Jobs at Apple.

The government can be an insurer for three years on new products. That might cause liability even though reasonable care has been exercised.

We need to encourage business firms to do research and development by making it tax deductible. It could come under a national payroll tax as a substitute for paying the tax.

We need to encourage more collaboration between universities and manufacturing firms. There should be a fund to provide for a year's salary to executives who go to engineering school or science programs for a year. Also, there should be a year's salary for professors who go to work for a manufacturing company. This facilitates a sharing of ideas.

There should be more mentoring in universities of graduate students who express an interest in doing inventive activities rather than developing theory. That might also involve some kind of a scholarship fund specifically for graduate students who have an interest in innovation technology.

It is important for inventors to work together in brainstorming ways. That could be encouraged through interdisciplinary programs, although they are often more theoretical than practical such as astrophysics.

II. OTHER C+ ARTICLES ON SUBJECT-SPECIFIC CREATIVITY

For further thoughts on how to encourage creativity technology, this is an exercise in creativity to think up creative thoughts. We thought up creative thoughts for the following articles that we can look back at to see what kind of general framework we used.

1. The first one I see is "Artistic Creativity" in Winter 2000. That depends on what kind of articles we are talking about.
2. We had plenty of articles on policy creativity such as creative legislation in autumn 2000 and all the articles that deal with "Government Innovation." They do not talk about how to encourage creativity. They talk more about examples like performance pay, vouchers, contracting out, competition. The one on legislation has a section called "Causes of Creative Legislation." It mentions political parties, personalities, crisis situations, social forces and academics. We are talking about public policies to encourage creativity.
3. "Business Creativity" in Spring 2001.
4. "Academic Creativity" in Spring 2001.

III. CAUSES OF CREATIVITY IN GENERAL

In order to talk about how to encourage creativity in technology, we should think about how to encourage creativity in general and then reason by analogy or deduction to technology. That means encouraging by way of public policy, although it is all right to talk about other causes.

A. Societal Causes

1. Free speech and press
2. Education and training
3. Libraries and information
4. Rewards like royalties and honors
5. Preschool socialization
6. Laboratories, think tanks, and conferences

All those are applicable to encouraging creativity in technology even though they are presented in the logo in the abstract.

B. The Individual Level

1. Ego Involvement
2. Risk taking
3. Willingness to have failures
4. Independence
5. Middle class
6. Intelligence

Public policy can encourage the growth of the middle class. This happens as result of automation which wipes out manual labor. That is the basis of the traditional working class. The middle class people work in offices, not in coal mines or factories, i.e., traditional laboring factories rather than automated factories.

The first four are highly subject to childhood socialization. Public policy can play a part in dividing daycare programs, nursery schools, kindergartens, elementary schools. Public policy can encourage socialization of values. Instead of ego involvements, it is personal responsibility. Independence is basically a can do attitude. Not necessarily. One can have a can do attitude but recognize the value of working with other people. Likewise, one can be a hermit and have a can=t do attitude. Meaning just being independent is not the same thing as being can do.

C. Tools That Facilitate Creativity

Other causes relate to having access to tools that facilitate creativity. All this is nicely summarized on page 39 of Winter 2000.

1. How to do it lists
2. Inspirational aids
3. Other people
4. Creativity-aiding software
5. Sleep, food exercise, and health aids
6. Flexible organization

If we list all 18 of those points in talking about encouraging creative technology, then we are a bit redundant to the more abstract causes of creativity. We could still list them across, not down. It would provide an opportunity for reviewing what we have said already.

IV. TRYING TO GENERALIZE FROM CREATIVE INVENTORS

We have six inventors in the computer room at the MKM-PSO-DSI Center. The title is Creative Inventions including Gutenberg, Watt, Bell, Edison, Ford, and Bill

Gates. None of them are scientists in the sense of having a Ph.D. degree or being professors. They are people with a practical orientation who made use of whatever science had already been developed. They were all people who are present at the right time, maybe also the right place. Four of the six are Americans, one is British, and Gutenberg I think was Dutch.

A. Time Period

Knowing where these people are from is relevant to understanding creative technology. When Gutenberg lived in Holland at about the time of the Renaissance, Holland was in the forefront of creativity, unlike the inquisition of Italy, Spain, and to some extent France, and the stifling culture of Eastern Europe. Holland welcomed Jews like Spinoza from Spain and Portugal. Holland was one of the first of the exploring countries with the Dutch East Indies which later became Indonesia and Dutch Guyana which later became Surinam. Britain was also doing well about then at the time of Queen Elizabeth. The Protestant countries had more religious freedom and encouraged work ethic and business entrepreneurship. The United States was a logical extension of Britain in that regard with some small Dutch influence in New York City.

B. Place or Country

On the matter of place, a country moving up as the United States was is a country that is likely to encourage inventiveness. The U.S. was certainly moving up.

The European discovery that lead to some settlement was 1492. That was largely Spain and Portugal and Brazil. Not much of an influence. In fact, one could say that Columbus was a leftover from pre-Ferdinand and Isabella. They created a stifling orthodoxy that did not survive after Columbus. Spain went down the drain when they were defeated by democratic England at the defeat of the Armada by Sir Francis Drake.

In 1620, about 150 years later, the British settled at Plymouth. In 1607, they settled at Jamestown. That was the real beginning of the United States. Real in the sense of the entrepreneurial spirit. Openness to science and intellect, religious tolerance, and openness to immigration. Those are the characteristics that have made the U.S. great for almost 400 years since 1620.

About a 100 years later, about 1720, the U.S. asserted its independence, more like 150 years later, in 1776, although the French and Indian War was good training for overthrowing an oppressive monarchy. It looks like every 150 years, the U.S. undergoes a big change. It took 150 years after 1492 and then 150 years after 1620.

Events happen closer together as a result of geometric progressions and exponential change. Thus big things were happening in the U.S. faster than 150 years from 1776. Although maybe not. Maybe the U.S. was rather stagnant from 1776 until at least 100 years after the Civil War when the Industrial Revolution really began in the U.S. with the opening of the Western Frontier, meaning California. The Gold Rush of 1849 was a bunch of prospectors, not settlers. The wave of settlers came after the Civil War. That's internal change though from east to west. The really big change came in the 1890s with waves of immigrants from Ireland, Italy, Poland, and Eastern Europe. These are people who came not so much to get rich like the gold rush prospectors but came to save up for sending their children to college of maybe their grandchildren if their children were born in Europe rather than the U.S. Those grandchildren are the lawyers, doctors, professors, and business executives of today. Some of them are inventors which is what we are talking about. That includes medical technology like the Salk and Sabin vaccines. It includes computer technologies. Also television which means the cathode ray tube which is essential to computers.

V. BUILDING ON PRIOR TECHNOLOGY

A lot of current new technology is really just an extension of technology of 100 years ago. The fax and Internet are basically extensions of the telephone. The computer is a combination of a calculator and a television set, not much has changed in automobiles, trains, boats, or even airplanes since Wilbur Wright. We also are still using the same forms of energy that Mr. Watt developed, mainly coal burning devices, although we use more electrical energy now rather than mechanical energy. Lighting isn=t much different than Edison invented 100 years ago. Thus what we have is a fantastic technological revolution that is not based on totally new science. Instead it is a new synthesis of old ideas.

The key element is the computer which synthesizes a whole bunch of things.

1. It synthesizes the typewriter. That is what the keyboard is.
2. It synthesizes the television set, that is what the monitor is.
3. It synthesizes a calculator. That is basically how it make computations.
4. It synthesizes a telephone. That is where the Internet comes in which is nothing but a telephone connection to a server rather than to the local grocery store. There may be a telephone connection to a store called Amazon.com. One has to dial its website number.
5. That is one of the reasons why it's hard to say who invented the computer because it really was invented by Mr. Scholes who invented the typewriter, Mr. DeForest who invented the TV set, Mr. Babbage who invented the calculator, and Mr. Bell who invented the telephone. Mr. Gates, whose picture is on the wall, is a business person rather than an engineer. He marketed the DOS system, which was invented by some unknown person he bought the idea from. Mr. Jobs had an alternative DOS system that seems to be going nowhere because it is locked into Apple hardware.

VI. SUMMARIZING GENERAL CHARACTERISTICS

A. Free Countries

The six inventors lived in countries that encouraged questioning, skepticism, and complaints about things not going as well as they could. Cultures that were not stifling, where people are expected to take the occupations of their fathers and grandfathers. The U.S. has been great on upward mobility largely because of immigrants coming in at the bottom. Those inventors were not immigrants. They were all pretty much native born Americans. Bell may have been born in Scotland but that is not very different from England and the U.S. as of 1850.

B. Moderately Well Educated

We mentioned already that they were moderately educated but not scientists or professors who may be too theoretical to invent a telephone. Although electricity theory was important to Bell, Edison, even Ford for starting a car and providing headlights and certainly Bill Gates. All computers run on electricity, at least batteries.

C. Good Monetary Rewards

All of them got good monetary rewards by virtue of being associated with implementing companies like Bell Telephone, Commonwealth Edison, Ford Motor Company, Microsoft. That is something worth noting. One could argue that they did it out of intellectual curiosity and the money came in almost accidentally. That does not seem to be so. They all had good business skills for implementing their ideas. This is in contrast to scientists like Einstein who never made any money off of nuclear energy, which he in effect invented. Marie Curie never made any money off of radiation therapy which she in effect invented. Scientists are motivated by intellectual curiosity. Inventors seem to be more motivated by making money. Monopolistic patents, though, restrict distribution. Receiving royalties, regardless who does the manufacturing, enabled Bill Gates to make a lot of money and still have widespread distribution.

VII. OTHER C+ ARTICLES ON TECHNOLOGY CREATIVITY

Another source of ideas on creativity and technology is to look at what other people have said on the subject that we have already published in the *Creativity Plus Journal*. Maybe only one such article. The one on Nobel Laureates as scientists not inventors. The one by Lewis called "Money as Netscape Motivator" gets at the money element.

1. "Money as Netscape Motivator" by Lewis.
2. Druker on "Systematic Entrepreneurship" talks about business creativity, not technology creativity.
3. The article on technology creativity by Sloan on page 37 of autumn 2000. Some of his points are:
    a. Necessity is the mother of invention. He adds though that it takes more than necessity. We do need a cure for AIDS and the common cold and don't have a cure. He says that three additional things are needed.
    b. First comes knowledge. We mentioned that those inventors were reasonably well educated, but not Ph.D.s. They had to know at least the undergraduate level of some physics and chemistry.
    c. Technical capacity. That refers to having equipment, like a laboratory, parts. That's where maybe a middle class element comes in because that costs money.
    d. Creative insight. Here he talks about trial and error, which gets at personality characteristics, like perseverance. We call that willingness to accept failure and keep going. I disagree with Sloan, though, partly in talking about inventions being the result of an accident.

VIII. FORTHCOMING TECHNOLOGICAL INNOVATIONS

It is difficult to predict what specific technological innovations are going to occur in the next generation or the next century. The journal of the World Futures Society frequently makes specific predictions.

It is much easier to predict in what fields of technology, innovations are likely to occur. One can with some degree of certainty. If the fields are broad enough, one can predict with some degree of certainty that there will be substantial innovation over the next 100 years in the following fields of technology:

1. TRANSPORTATION including automobiles, airplanes, ships, rockets, trains, buses, and maybe individual systems of transportation rather than group systems.
2. COMMUNICATION including radio, TV, E-mail, Internet, faxing, regular mail and phoning. Phoning includes regular mail, stationary phones and portable cell phones.
3. ENERGY PRODUCTION including massive solar energy, safer forms of nuclear energy, fusion energy using hydrogen, fusion energy using

helium and especially changes in the economics of energy production including the required renting out of infrastructures.

4. PUBLISHING words including word processing, printing presses, photocopying, high speed computer printers, and other ways of producing and duplicating text.

5. REPRODUCING PICTURES including camcorders, videotape players, DVD tape players, digitized photography, and ways of sending pictures and movies electronically.

6. REPRODUCING SOUND including magnetic tapes, CDs, DVDs, and ways of downloading music and sound tracks that facilitate distribution while providing incentives to create new music.

7. LIGHTING including incandescent lamps, neon lights, halogen lamps, computerized lighting displays, massive lighting from small bulbs, and longer lasting bulbs.

8. COMPUTERS including improvements in speed of processing and in storage capacity. Also responsiveness to voice commands, although that is getting into software rather than hardware.

9. SOFTWARE for aiding in arriving at decisions or in stimulating creativity. Also software that can improve upon existing software for office practice, information retrieval, spreadsheets, word processing, file management, document assembly, running factories, military uses, mathematics, statistical analysis, etc.

10. MEDICAL technology, including (1) stem cell research for replacing defective tissues, (2) new diagnostic techniques with regard to CAT scans, sonograms, MRIs and new blood tests for cancer and other diseases, (3) new ways of treating cancer, diabetes, heart disease, strokes, and other aging diseases, (4) new understanding about physical and psychological ways of improving immune systems, etc.

11. ANTI-POLLUTION technologies, including new ways dealing with agriculture, transportation, manufacturing, and energy production that are simultaneously more profitable and cleaner such as genetically improved agriculture, hybrid automobiles, non-toxic mining, and fusion or solar energy production mentioned above.

PART THREE:

PUBLIC POLICY CREATIVITY

Chapter 14

GOVERNMENT INNOVATION: PERFORMANCE PAY, VOUCHERS, AND CONTRACTING OUT

This is the fourth in a series of articles dealing with government innovation in *Creativity Plus*. The first article appeared in the Spring 2000 issue and dealt with "Win-Win Performance Pay." The examples included:

1. Paying stock brokers a percentage of the dividends and/or resale profits.
2. Giving manufacturers an incentive to adopt cleaner processes by making those processes more profitable.
3. Paying employment agencies commissions after welfare recipients have been on the job for at least a few months.
4. Providing bonuses to police officers based on percentage of crimes solved by police units and individual officers.

The second article appeared in the Summer 2000 issue and dealt with "Win-Win Vouchers." The examples included:

1. Vouchers to cover the difference between a sub-minimum wage and a minimum wage, provided that the employer offers on-the-job training to bring the worker up to at least the minimum wage level.
2. Vouchers to cover the difference between what workers can afford to pay for food and what farmers need to supply the food, provided that both the workers and the farmers upgrade their productivity.
3. Housing vouchers to get inner-city residents to move up one concentric circle in economic neighborhoods so that their children will go to better schools.
4. Training vouchers to be used by any adult to upgrade his or her productivity through training, but the vouchers cannot be redeemed unless the trainee passes a test and can be redeemed in double if the trainee obtains a new job for at least six months.

The third article appeared in the Autumn 2000 issue and dealt with "Win-Win Contracting Out." The examples included:

1.   Contracting out state factories or state farms with provisions for protecting workers, consumers, and the environment or else the contract is terminated or not renewed.
2.   Contracting out legal services for the poor with provisions for law reform activities, clarifying and enforcing existing rights, affirmative recruitment, public education, seeking legislation, law school interaction, and the writing of the appropriate articles and books.
3.   Contracting out prisons with specifications that they should be operated at 80% of former cost and the recidivism rate should be improved by at least 10%.
4.   Contracting out some or all of the public schools with provisions requiring cost reduction rather than production, test score improvement, and integration.

The purpose of this article is to provide further illustrations of win-win performance pay, vouchers, and contracting out.

I. MORE WIN-WIN PERFORMANCE PAY: HEALTH

The additional example of win-win performance pay relates to the use of health management organizations (HMO's) as a key part of healthcare policy. Medicare and Medicaid emphasize individuals who go to whatever doctor will service them, and then the government pays all or a high percentage of each case-by-case doctor bill. Such a system tends to be much more expensive than salaried government doctors and is inequitable if it only covers the poor and the aged.

Government-owned hospitals or salaried government doctors tend to be inefficient due to lack of competition. Such a system is also inequitable if it only applies to veterans or poor people since health care expenses can no longer be easily afforded by lower middle-class people or middle-class people in general.

Subsidized HMO's in this context means the government provides health care vouchers to poor people, aged people, and middle-class people who can qualify. Such vouchers supplement the premiums which HMO's require in order to provide HMO coverage. The HMO's compete with each other, thereby generating lower prices and better quality service. The money for the vouchers can come mainly from employers to cover their own employees, with a provision for covering the self-employed and the non-employed. See Table 1.

II. MORE WIN-WIN VOUCHERS: SCHOOLS

When people think of vouchers in the school policy context, they think of vouchers that will support parochial and private schools at the expense of public schools. This is not necessarily the case.

Privatization can be either conservative if private companies are paid to achieve conservative goals, or it can be liberal if private companies are paid to achieve liberal goals.

Table 2 shows the school vouchers situation in a win-win context. Conservatives tend to favor vouchers for elementary and high school. Doing so will save taxpayer money by diverting students away from the public schools with private and parochial schools absorbing some of the costs. Such schools will also be more disciplined.

Liberals object to vouchers for elementary and high schools. They argue in favor of using the money for inner-city public schools. Their goal is to improve inner-city learning and to preserve the public school system.

A win-win voucher system might provide for government vouchers to attend non-governmental schools including those that may be run by the parochial school system. If they are run by the parochial school system, they must be in buildings that have no religious orientation such as crucifixes on the walls. The teachers must also be either non-priests or non-nuns or possibly some priests and nuns wearing secular clothing.

Such a system could be a win-win system. It would save taxpayer money especially if the secular schools run by the parochial school systems agree to a tuition rate per student that is less than what it costs per student to educate them in the public school system. While getting costs down, the learning quality could go up as a result of (1) more experienced teachers who are willing to teach in the inner-city schools, (2) salaries based on performance rather than union seniority, and (3) a more disciplined atmosphere. Those learning quality factors could appeal to both conservatives and liberals especially when there is no breach of separation of church and state as there would be in vouchers to parochial schools.

Table 1. Health Care Policy

GOALS ALTERNATIVES	C Privatization	L Equity
C Marketplace or Medicare + and Medicaid	+	−
L Government-owned hospitals	−	+
N Both	0	0
SOS OR WIN-WIN Subsidized HMO's	++	++

Table 2. Vouchers for Secular-Parochial Schools

GOALS ALTERNATIVES	C Save taxpayer money More disciplined schools	L Improve inner-city education learning
C Vouchers for elementary and high schools	+	−
L No vouchers for elementary and high schools Using the money for inner-city public schools	−	+
SOS OR WIN-WIN Vouchers for secular inner-city schools run by the parochial school system	++	++

III. MORE WIN-WIN CONTRACTING OUT: SOLID WASTE

Conservatives tend to favor privatization in sold waste collection, in order to increase individual responsibility and reduce taxes. Liberals tend to favor government collection with recycling, in order to increase community responsibility and provide for a cleaner environment.

A compromise is to provide for contracting out by the city government. That is better from a conservative viewpoint than solid waste collection by government employees, but not so good as having each residence or business arrange for solid waste collection. Contracting out is better from a liberal viewpoint than total privatization because the government is in control of who will get the contract and what the contract provisions will be more than if the government tries to regulate the solid waste collectors, but not as much as the government doing the collecting itself.

An SOS solution would be one that reduces the cost of the contract and provides for an even cleaner environment by preventing the solid waste form coming into existence or needing collection. That can be done by giving homeowners and businesses vouchers to buy various kinds of equipment and services that will reduce the need for solid waste collection. An example would be a voucher for buying a mulcher for one's lawnmower to reduce the need for grass collection. Another example would be a voucher for buying a tin-can compactor, which substantially reduces the cost and expense of collecting and recycling tin cans.

The 1994 experience of Champaign indicates that regulated privatization may be more of an SOS alternative than contracting out. The regulation requires private haulers to pick up recyclables. If recycling is purely voluntary, it does not get done so well. The regulation also requires every business firm and household to arrange for hauling of garbage and recyclables. That is a mix of liberal regulation with private enterprise doing the work. The government is in control, but the contracting out is by business firms and households.

Table 3. Solid Waste Collection

GOALS ALTERNATIVES	C Individual responsibility Reduce taxes	L Community responsibility Clean environment
C Privatization	+	−
L Government collection with recycling	−	+
N Contracting out	0	0
SOS OR WIN-WIN Vouchers to reduce solid waste Contracting out	++	++

IV. SOME CONCLUSIONS

This series of four articles has illustrated that win-win performance pay, win-win vouchers, and win-win contracting out can be a useful form of government innovation. They are useful in the sense that they are geared toward enabling both conservatives and liberals to come out ahead of their best initial expectations simultaneously. Ordinary performance pay, vouchers, and contracting out tend to be geared more toward conservative privatization, especially with regard to contracting out, or toward liberal vouchers which may be a form of welfare handouts, like food stamps. Performance pay tends to be either conservative or liberal depending on whether people are being paid to perform conservative or liberal goals.

As part of our desire to get readers of *Creativity Plus* more involved in an interactive way with this journal of the Policy Studies Organization, we would like to invite readers to suggest other forms of win-win performance pay, win-win vouchers, and win-win contracting out. There may be many more government activities and goals that could benefit from this kind of useful innovation, but the applications have not been made or even suggested. These are new and useful ways of thinking about governmental activity. If two heads are better than one, then 1,200 PSO thinkers should be better than two, without too many cooks spoiling the chicken soup for the creative soul.

Chapter 15

GOVERNMENT INNOVATION: WIN-WIN CONTRACTING OUT

I. SOCIALISM VERSUS CAPITALISM

The changes that are occurring in Eastern Europe and in many other regions and nations of the world provide an excellent opportunity to apply systematic policy analysis to determining such basic matters as how to organize the economy, the government, and other social institutions. Population control and land reform are highly important problems, but they may not be as basic as reconstituting a society.

Table 1 analyzes the fundamental issue of socialism versus capitalism in the context of government versus private ownership and operation of the basic means of producing industrial and agricultural products. The essence of socialism in this context is government ownership and operation of factories and farms or at least those larger than the handicraft or garden-size, as in the Soviet Union of 1960. The essence of capitalism is private ownership and operation of both factories and farms, as in the United States of 1960. The neutral position or middle way is to have some government and some private ownership-operation, as in Sweden of 1960. The year 1960 is used because that is approximately when the Soviet Union began to change with the advent of Nikita Khrushchev. The United States also underwent big changes in the 1960s with the advent of John F. Kennedy.

Table 1 refers to government ownership-operation as the liberal or left-wing alternative, as it is in the United States and in world history at least since the time of Karl Marx. The table refers to private ownership-operation as the conservative or right-wing alternative, as it is in the U.S., and elsewhere at least since the time of Adam Smith. In recent years in the Soviet Union and in China, those favoring privatization have been referred to as liberals, and those favoring retention of government ownership-operation have been referred to as conservatives. The labels make no difference in this context. The object of Table 1 is to find a super-optimum solution that more than satisfies the goals of both ideologies or groups, regardless of their labels.

The key capitalistic goal is high productivity in terms of income-producing goods substantially above what it costs to produce them. The key socialistic goal is equity in terms of the sharing of ownership, operation, wealth, and income. Other goals that tend to be more socialistic than capitalistic, but are less fundamental consist of (1) workplace quality, including wages, hours, safety, hiring by merit, and worker input, (2) environmental protection, including reduction of air, water, radiation, noise, and other forms of pollution, and (3) consumer protection, including low prices and goods that are durable, safe, and high quality.

Going down the productivity column, the liberal socialistic alternative does not score so high on productivity for a lack of profit-making incentives and a surplus of bureaucratic interference in comparison to the capitalistic alternative, assuming the level of technology is held constant. The empirical validity of that statement is at least partially confirmed by noting that the capitalistic countries of Japan and West Germany are more productive than their socialistic counterparts of East Germany and China, although they began at approximately the same level as of 1945 at the end of World War II. Going down the equity column, the liberal socialistic alternative does score relatively high. By definition, it involves at least a nominal collective sharing in the ownership and operation of industry and agriculture, which generally leads to less inequality in wealth and income than capitalism does.

On the goals that relate to the workplace, the environment, and consumers, the socialists traditionally argue that government ownership-operation is more sensitive to those matters because it is less profit oriented. The capitalists traditionally argue that private ownership-operation is more sensitive in competitive marketplaces in order to find quality workers and to increase the quantity of one's consumers. The reality (as contrasted to the theory is that without alternative incentives or regulations, both government managers and private managers of factories and farms are motivated toward high production at low cost. That kind of motivation leads to cutting back on the expenses of providing workplace quality, environmental protection, and consumer protection. The government factory manager of the Polish steelworks may be just as abusive of labor as the private factory manager for the US Steel Company. Likewise, the government factory managers in the state factories of China may be just as insensitive to consumer safety and durability as their monopolistic counterparts in the American automobile industry.

As for how the super-optimum solution operates, it involves government ownership, but all the factories and farms are rented to private entrepreneurs to develop productive and profitable manufacturing and farming. Each lease is renewable every year, or longer if necessary to get productive tenants. A renewal can be refused if the factory or farm is not being productively developed, or if the entrepreneur is not showing adequate sensitivity to workers, the environment, and consumers.

As for some of the advantages of such an SOS system, it is easier to not renew a lease than it is to issue injunctions, fines, jail sentences, or other negative sanctions. It is also much less expensive than subsidies. The money received for rent can be an important source of tax revenue for the government to provide productive subsidies elsewhere in the economy. Those subsidies can be especially used for encouraging technological innovation-diffusion, the upgrading of skills, and stimulating competition for market share which can be so much more beneficial to society than either socialistic or capitalistic monopolies. The government can more easily demand sensitivity to workers, the environment, and consumers from its renters of factories and farms than it can from itself. There is a conflict of interest in regulating oneself.

This SOS alternative is only available to socialistic countries like the USSR, China, Cuba, North Korea, and others since they already own the factories and land. It would not be economically or politically feasible for capitalistic countries to move from the conservative capitalistic alternative to the SOS solution by acquiring ownership through payment or confiscation. This is an example where socialistic countries are in a position to decide between socialism and capitalism by compromising and winding up with the worst of both possible worlds. That means the relative unproductivity of socialism and the relative inequity of capitalism. The socialistic countries are also in a position to decide between the two basic alternatives by winding up with the best of both possible worlds. That means retaining the equities and social sensitivities of government ownership, while having the high productivity that is associated with profit-seeking entrepreneurial capitalism. It would be difficult to find a better example of compromising versus super-optimizing than the current debate over socialism versus capitalism.

The third problem is the privatization problem. It illustrates how two apparently conflicting approaches can be simultaneously combined with a somewhat imaginative combination that is not a compromise. It is a combination where both sides do better than their best expectations rather than yield substantially to the other side. Other examples include:

1. The example of legal services for the poor with volunteers absorbed into the salaried system through a well organized clearinghouse and training program.
2. Combining private enterprise and state enterprise in American higher education within the same schools as well as in the system.

Table 1. Government versus Private Ownership and Operation

GOALS ALTERNATIVES	C High Productivity	L 1. Equity 2. Workplace Quality 3. Environmental Protection 4. Consumer Protection
C Private Ownership and Operation (Capitalism)	+	–
L Government Ownership and Operation (Socialism)	–	+
N Some Government and Some Private	0	0
SOS OR WIN-WIN 100% Government Own 100% Private Operation	++	++

II. ATTORNEYS FOR THE POOR

The Washington newsletter of the American Bar Association reports that Legal Services Corporation was given a five-year authorization during the Bush Administration.

A. Progressive Contracting Out of Legal Services

The idea of competitive bidding or contracting out of legal services raises some interesting questions. One question is simply whether it is possible for a Democratic Congress to trust a Republican administration with handling competitive bidding. In theory, this could be a highly liberal kind of privatization. The specification of the contract on which bids are taken could be like the following:

1. Law reform. Whoever gets the contract must agree to devote half their money to law reform cases before the Supreme Court or other courts. Such cases are designed to improve substantially the legal rights of the poor as consumers, tenants, welfare recipients, public housing recipients, voters, arrested persons, employees, health care recipients, students in elementary and high schools, family members, clients of lawyers and other frequent roles.
2. Clarifying and enforcing existing rights. Perhaps more important than improving rights is just seeking clarification and enforcement of existing rights.
3. Affirmative recruitment. A strong affirmative action program must be adopted to seek out qualified lawyers who are women, members of minorities, disabled, from poor backgrounds and so on. The affirmative action program should not award any preference or points to those people. The emphasis should be on affirmatively seeking out those who are qualified.
4. Public education. There should be a lot of public education in the contract, informing the general public about the legal rights of the poor and the legal rights of consumers, tenants and so on, regardless of whether they are poor.
5. Seeking legislation. The contract should include active activities on the part of the firm that is awarded the contract in terms of seeking legislation designed to better clarify and enforce the legal rights of the poor, and not just court cases.
6. Law school interaction. There should be activity at law schools across the country designed to bring law students into the program according to the theory that this will give them an involvement that will carry on for the rest of their lives and help to shape favorably their attitudes toward legal services for the poor.
7. Writing articles and book. In addition to counseling activities, litigation activities, legislative activities, law reform and negotiation, there should be encouragement of activities that involve the writing of law review articles or books. This is more a matter of educating the bar and influencing the legal system than it is of public education.

In other words, just because the system is turned over to private enterprise does not mean that poor people are going to be hurt. It all depends on what the contracting out provides for in the contract. If it has provisions like the above, it is much better than government ownership and operation. This is really a good example of cases where liberals have a knee-jerk negative reaction to privatization as somehow being inherently reactionary.

B. Progressive Contracting Out in General

Privatization does not mean an inherent conflict between government ownership and operation, and private ownership and operation. It can mean government ownership and private operation through a progressive system of contracting out, as contrasted to a reactionary system.

A progressive system involves contracting out with contract provisions requiring environmental protection, workplace safety and consumer protection. It also involves contracting out to more than one supplier of the service in order to provide competition. It further involves relatively short-term contracts that come up for renewal and are not renewed if they are not being complied with. Also there should be provisions in the contract for terminating it before the term is up if violations are severe enough.

A reactionary system involves contracting out leaving the private entrepreneur free to do anything they want with regard to the environment, workplace or consumers. Worse, they are given a monopolistic franchise that leads to even more abuses than would result from simply not having any contract provisions against them. It is also highly undesirable that the contract be for an indefinite time or a definite time that is so long, that the idea of non-renewal gets lost in inertia, or that the contract provide for a relatively short time but there is no monitoring of it to see if it is being well complied with, and renewal tends to be automatic.

The concept of contracting out normally refers to the reactionary version and therefore it tends to be opposed by liberals. A progressive version of contracting out, though, can be even better for promoting liberal values than government ownership and operation. The progressive version is also politically and administratively feasible. It is politically feasible because it represents a move away from government ownership and operation, which conservatives should endorse. It is politically feasible for liberals, given the liberal provisions. It is administratively feasible because there will be entrepreneurs who will be pleased to accept these contracting provisions if what they are supplying in the way of services or other activities involves substantially less expense on their part than what they are being paid to do. If the contract is highly profitable, they can easily absorb the environment, workplace and consumer provisions.

Even though the entrepreneurs are making a profit, the government and taxpayer may also be coming out well ahead. This is so because the private entrepreneur may be reducing expenses through the incentive of competition and the private profit motive. These incentives may also be substantially improving the quality of what is being provided, beyond what a monopolistic government agency could provide.

A recent new form of contracting out is the running of the public schools in a city or school district by private enterprise firm. The contract provides that the firm receives payment equal to 90 per cent of the previous tax costs. The contract also provides for various standards designed to determine how well the students are learning at the beginning of the contract and at the end of each academic year. The contract can be awarded through open bidding, and is up for renewal or rebidding every few years. This arrangement may improve the quality of the schools, but generally does nothing for the integration of students from different economic classes.

III. PRIVATE-SECTOR PRISONS

On the contracting-out of prisons, the conservative way is to do it. The liberal way is don't do it. The neutral way is do it some. The conservative goal is to increase profits to business and reduce costs to the taxpayers. The liberal goal is to be nice to prisoners, or at least don't mistreat them simply to cut expenses and raise profits. The SOS or Win-Win solution is a contract that says the private sector company must run the prison at 80% of the former cost and improve the recidivism rate by 10%, or they lose the contract. Improving profits satisfies the conservatives. Reducing recidivism appeals especially to liberals. The contract could also have a provision whereby the contracting business firm loses the contract if it fails to comply with the provisions, including open bidding, not abusing the workers, and not abusing the environment.

Table 2. Contracting Out Prisons

CRITERIA ALTERNATIVES	C More Profits Less Taxes	L No Mistreatment
C Do It	+	−
L Don't Do It	−	+
N Do It some	0	0
SOS Contract Provisions: 1. 80% of Former Cost 2. Improved Recidivism Rate by 10% 3. Open Auction Bidding with Termination for Cause	++	++

IV. CONTRACTING OUT PUBLIC SCHOOLS

Table 3 deals with education policy at the kindergarten through twelfth grade level. The problem especially relates to school integration and the need to uplift inner-city schools. The conservative position is basically to do nothing, on the grounds that things are fine the way they are, or as good as they reasonably can be. The key conservative goal is to support the neighborhood school system. Many conservatives would also like to see more support for private schools, including possibly religious private schools.

The liberals have since about 1960 been advocating busing to bring inner-city students to integrated and better schools. Their goal is integration and support from the public school system.

The neutral position is partial busing which could mean (1) only short distances, (2) only within the city limits, and (3) only busing out of the inner-city, no busing in. It is also a neutral position to advocate spending more money on inner-city schools to compensate for their relatively low-quality buildings, lack of experienced teachers, and middle-class peer group inspiration.

A recent new alternative is contracting out the running of the public schools in a city or school district to a private enterprise firm. The contract provides that the firm receives payment equal to 90 percent of the previous tax costs. The contract also provides for various standards designed to determine how well the students are learning at the beginning of the contract and at the end of each academic year. The contract can be awarded through open bidding, and is up for renewal or rebidding every few years. This arrangement may improve the quality of the schools, but generally does nothing for economic-class integration of the students. It thus needs supplementing with policies like (1) rent vouchers that must be used one concentric circle up in terms of the economic status of the neighborhoods and (2) setting aside former public housing land for integrated condominium developments near downtown employment.

Table 3. Education Policy, Especially Integration

GOALS ALTERNATIVES	C 1. Neighborhood schools 2. Private schools	L 1. Integration 2. Public schools
C Do Nothing	+	−
L Busing	−	+
N 1. Integration-oriented rent subsidies 2. Contracting out	++	++

Chapter 16

GOVERNMENT INNOVATION: COMPETITION

This is the fifth in a series of articles on "Government innovation" appearing in the quarterly journal called Creativity Plus. The previous four articles emphasized samples of win-win policy analysis applied to (1) win-win performance pay, (2) win-win vouchers, (3) win-win contracting out, and (4) a combination of all three innovative ideas.

The present article provides six examples of government innovation in the context of win-win competition as applied to the six major policy fields of:

1. Economic policy: competition among business firms, especially electricity and communications
2. Technology policy: competition among inventors, especially licensing with royalties rather than monopolistic patents
3. Social policy- competition among and within schools
4. Political policy: competition among and within political parties
5. International policy: competition among countries in the selling of goods and services
6. Legal policy: competition among and within police forces to reduce crime.

I. PUBLIC POLICY TOWARD BUSINESS FIRMS

The conservative alternative of an unregulated marketplace may lead to only one or a few firms dominating most industries. That arrangement may be profitable in the short run, although contrary to low prices. The liberal alternative of government ownership or tight regulation tends to mean a government monopoly or stifled private enterprise. That means reduced business profits, although it might mean artificially low prices to satisfy consumers as voters. The mixed economy scores in the middle on both business profits and low prices.

The SOS alternative may draw upon the stimulus to innovation and efficiency of private profit making. The SOS alternative may encourage competition through well placed seed money and other competition facilitators. Doing so results in lower prices through a competitive marketplace, rather than through a monopolistic one or through artificial price constraints.

The marketplace is associated with capitalism. It may not be associated with competition if the marketplace leads to monopolies or firms working together to decrease competition. Regulation or government ownership is associated with socialism. It is even more likely to lead to monopoly, but monopoly in the hands of the state rather than private enterprise. The marketplace may lead to better business profits than regulation does. Regulation may lead to better consumer prices than the marketplace does.

An SOS alternative is competition which is likely to lead to even better total business profits than the marketplace, although not necessarily better profits for each firm. Competition is likely to lead to better consumer prices and quality of products than regulation. Competition can be stimulated through laws that (1) require licensing of patents and facilities, (2) lowering of tariffs to increase international competition, and (3) seed money to get new businesses established or expanded to make an industry more competitive, and (4) require leasing of networks of electricity, telephone, and cable-TV.

II. PUBLIC POLICY TOWARD INVENTORS

Preserving the patent system (as it is currently operating) tends to stifle some creativity by providing for a 17-year monopoly renewable once, but frequently renewed repeatedly with slight variations. It also stifles creativity by being the basis for lawsuits designed to obtain injunctions against creative competition.

Abolishing patents can hurt some creativity on the part of people who develop new inventions in order to obtain a monopolistic patent, although as of 1999 those new inventions may be for relatively small matters, rather than for new forms of transportation, communication, energy, or health care.

Changing the system by shortening the patent monopoly, requiring licensing, or having the government as an insurer against product liability can be helpful, but not as much as well-placed subsidies to encourage needed inventions.

Well-placed subsidies could mean calling a conference of leading scientists and engineers to develop a list of 50-100 important needed inventions. The government could then announce the availability of grants and other monetary rewards to encourage the development of those inventions. The rewards could be worth more than a monopolistic patent while encouraging (rather than stifling) competition.

III. PUBLIC POLICY TOWARD SCHOOLS

Public school education can be made more competitive in the following ways:

1. More competition among teachers with salary rewards for quality work or for working in neighborhoods where teachers are reluctant to work.
2. More competition among students for academic honors and less competition for sports honors.
3. More competition among school districts by publicizing how well school districts are doing on SAT scores, college entrance percentages, and other variables, including publicity over time so that they are in effect competing with their past.
4. Rent supplements and anti-snob zoning laws in order to facilitate people voting with their feet by moving to better school districts more easily.
5. Conservatives talk about vouchers that would enable public school children to go to private schools. That is not an example of competition to improve quality. It is frequently motivated by any results in pure racism and economic class bias.
6. A voucher system could be meaningful to enable public school children to pay transportation costs and school lunch costs to attend a public school in the middle class neighborhoods of their district, or even outside their district. That is an example of a use of vouchers to promote integration rather than to promote private school, racism or private school religious fundamentalism or parochial Catholic schools under the guise of competition to promote quality.
7. We could also talk about competition at the higher education level, which gets into regional and international competition. One of the best ways the government", can promote competition among universities or among business firms is to publicize how well each producer is doing on various objective criteria so as to embarrass many universities in the United States that lay people think are good universities such as expensive private universities, the military academies, religious schools. Those universities are not likely to do very well on Nobel Prize winners, or even the percentage or quantity of people who go on to become doctors or lawyers or professors. Especially if one thinks in terms of benefit/cost ratios. The state universities would look much. better than the lay public thinks given the low tuition's and the high results in terms of various quality indicators.

IV. PUBLIC POLICY TOWARD POLITICAL PARTIES

1. This is a totally different area in which to encourage competition. Here it definitely does not make sense to say we will contract out to business firms to set up political parties.
2. The device that is sometimes advocated for getting more competition among parties is proportional representation rather than single-member districts where only a major or dominant political party can win.

Proportional representation provides too much diffusion and gives too much power to small swing parties in forming a ruling condition.

3. Free speech is very important in developing opposition which develops opposition Political parties. That means no restrictions on political communication with regard to content.

4. There may have to be restrictions on spending so as to prevent one party from spending itself into a monopolistic position. The best way to deal with that is through government financing of elections which pays the costs of both the incumbent party and the opposition, as well as other major parties if there are any.

5. The government can provide facilities for political parties that are capable of getting at least ten percent or so of the vote. The facilities can include a speaking hall, radio time, TV time. The object is to subsidize the low-income parties that are not minor splinter parties but are major viewpoints as indicated by the percentage of votes they are capable of getting but would not be very competitive without a subsidy, which the dominant party does not need. This would not run contrary to majority rule. The minority party would still have to convince voters that it is the better or best party in order to get elected.

6. Redistricting so as to give opposition parties a fair chance of getting represented in the legislature. That is the proportionate representation that goes with geography, not with saying that a party that gets one percent of the votes is entitled to one percent of the legislators.

7. Anything that increases registration and turnout is likely to increase political action and a diversity of major viewpoints. If only a relatively small portion of the population is registered and votes, that segment of the population in effect has a monopoly on running the government even though within that segment there may be more than one party.

The East German economy has been a relative failure compared to the West German economy since World War II. This has been used as a factor to show the superiority of capitalism over socialism. Some contrary evidence is the fact that the Swedish socialistic economy has flourished since World War II in spite of relatively few people and resources. The Spanish capitalistic economy has been a much greater failure than the East German socialistic economy since World War II. One can get much greater predictability out of knowing whether a society has a competitive economy and political system (versus a monopolistic one) than out of knowing whether it is a capitalistic private-ownership economy (or a socialistic government ownership economy).

Both East Germany and Spain have been failures in terms of providing high standards of living for their people. They both have one-party monopolistic political systems, although one was communist and the other was fascist. They both have monopolistic economic systems which try to keep out foreign goods through high tariffs. with government-favored business firms, although one had government-owned firms and the other had privately-owned firms.

Both West Germany and Sweden have been successes in terms of providing high standards of living for their people. They both have competitive political systems, with strong two-party competition, whereby the out-party is constantly trying to offer better ideas than the in-party. They both encourage competition among business firms and allow foreign competition. Thus comparing East Germany and West Germany does point to ways in which public policy can improve the quality of life, but it is a public policy that encourages competition over monopoly, not necessarily one that encourages capitalism over socialism.

V. PUBLIC POLICY TOWARD FREE TRADE

A. Improving International Competitiveness

The conservative position (as indicated in the Bush Administration) has been to emphasize that government regulation increases business expenses and thereby reduces international competitiveness.

The liberal position (as indicated in the Carter Administration) has been to emphasize the need to lower tariffs, break-up monopolies, and encourage more labor-management teamwork.

The neutral position has been to avoid substantial changes in regulation, tariffs, and other such controversies.

The SOS alternative (as indicated by some elements in the Clinton Administration) is to emphasize government investment in technological diffusion and the upgrading of skills. Doing so is capable of increasing the profits of business and the wages of labor. It can also result in better products at lower prices for both domestic and international markets.

B. The North American Free Trade Agreement and Tariffs

U.S. exporters and investors are helped by free trade with Mexico and other places because (1) Mexicans can buy more U.S. products if there are no Mexican tariffs artificially raising the price of American products, (2) Mexicans can buy more U.S. products if they have more income as a result of working in factories that have expanded as a result of American capital, and (3) U.S. investors can make money and add to the U.S. GNP by investing in Mexican factories which are now able to export better to the U.S. because U.S. tariffs have been dropped.

U.S. consumers are helped by free trade with Mexico and other places because (1) they can buy products made in Mexico at lower prices because they no longer have a U.S. tariff artificially raising the prices, (2) they can benefit from low prices that should result from decreased labor expenses associated with some products made in Mexico, possibly stimulated with American capital, and (3) U.S. consumers include business firms that buy producer goods less expensively from Mexico and thereby make American firms more internationally competitive.

U.S. firms and workers who are not sufficiently competitive would be hurt by the NAFTA agreement, but this can be minimized by (1) retraining workers and firms so they can be more competitive in their old products or new products, (2) side agreements with Mexico that require upgrading of labor standards in Mexico, and (3) disrupted workers and firms may benefit from the increased prosperity of the U.S. as a result of more exporting, better overseas investing, and better buys for U.S. consumers.

Mexicans can benefit in the same ways as Americans by just substituting for the three goal-columns (1) Mexican exporters and investors, (2) non-competitive Mexican firms and workers, and (3) Mexican consumers.

The opponents of NAFTA are referred to in this table as conservatives, and the advocates are referred to as liberals. That is done partly to simplify the calculation of the tools. It is also in accordance with the fact that conservatives have traditionally been in favor of high tariffs, although in recent years that is less true than from about 1800 through the 1930's.

VI. PUBLIC POLICY TOWARD POLICE ACTIVITIES

Competition with regard to police protection:

1. The first thing that comes to mind is hiring private police. That is all right for rich business firms. A ghetto dweller is not going to hire a private police company to protect his family from being burglarized and mugged.
2. As mentioned above, publicizing quality indicators for different police departments across the country or different police stations within a given city stimulates better output including quality indicators over time so that one competes with oneself the way a jogger tries to improve.
3. The rent supplement idea enables people who live in neighborhoods with bad police protection to move elsewhere more easily just as it enables people to move who live in neighborhoods with bad schools. Most of what is said above about competition among schools can also apply to police protection and other government services.
4. More competition among police officers for internal police department rewards such as salary increases, promotions, and honors.
5. In dealing with competition at the governmental service level, some of the methods that apply in the private sector may not be so applicable, but thinking about them might stimulate some applicable ideas such as contracting out to domestic or international business firms. This is not the same as a business firm hiring a private detective agency. What it means is that the city of Chicago would have the responsibility for

providing good police protection throughout the city, but instead of doing it through Chicago employees it might hire a professional agency if the agency or business firm can meet the specifications with regard to personnel and equipment. There would then be competition among such business firms to get the contracts. All contracts world be subject to renewal every year or so in order to make it clear that the contracts do not last forever regardless of a drop in the quality of service. It is quite possible that such a contracting out could lead to a more sensitive police operation in the inner city than is currently provided by an arrogant police force that in effect does have a contract forever.

Chapter 17

LEVERAGED PRODUCTIVITY CREDIT UNIONS

Previous issues of *Creativity Plus* have discussed creative ideas for new kinds of governmental institutions.

Those institutions have included:

1. Win-win performance pay, discussed in the Spring 2000 issue of *Creativity Plus* and the Winter 2000 issue
2. Win-win contracting out, discussed in the Autumn 2000 issue of *Creativity Plus* and the Winter 2000 issue
3. Win-win vouchers, discussed in the Summer 2000 issue of *Creativity Plus* and the Winter 2000 issue
4. Win-win competition, discussed in the Spring 2001 issue of *Creativity Plus*.

The purpose of this short article is to discuss a fifth new governmental institution that has win-win characteristics. Such characteristics can enable conservatives, liberals, and other major viewpoints to all come out ahead of their best initial expectations simultaneously.

I. FARM-WORKERS AND GROWERS

The new governmental institution can be called the leveraged productivity credit union. A good example is included in the settlement negotiations between the United Farm Workers and the Peoria Growers Association back in 1990.

The Union wanted $1,000,000 damages due to the failure of management to properly record rent and sales transactions from the company housing and stores. The Growers Association refused to pay even $1. The object of a win-win dispute resolution was to give the Union value worth more than $1,000,000 and make the Growers pay less than $1. That means the Growers should receive money, rather than pay.

The proposed solution was to establish a special credit union. The Growers would put up $500,000 which the credit union could use as collateral to borrow ten times that from the Department of Housing and Urban Development. With that $5,000,000, the credit union could loan money to build cooperative and condominium apartment buildings for the farm workers to live in as replacement for the company housing. The credit union could also loan money to start stores to replace the company stores.

The value of the housing and the stores in terms of money saved and satisfaction by the workers was more than $1,000,000. The Growers got their $500,000 back in five years with interest. They thus made money on their $500,000. They also were relieved of what they considered to be the burden of running company housing and company stores. They also received a promise by the union not to complain further about the Growers' failure to comply with the proper recording rules.

This is called a leveraged productivity credit union. The word "leveraged" is used because the credit union uses a relatively small amount of money to borrow a large amount of money, which it then turns around and lends to its borrowers. The word "productivity" is used because the money loaned can only be used for capital investment or for productivity, rather than for consumption goods like cars, refrigerators, or houses.

The word "credit union" is used, rather than "bank," because credit unions tend to be owned by the borrowers, rather than by bankers. The concept of a union also sounds more worker-friendly than the concept of a bank.

II. SCHOOL INFRASTRUCTURE BANKS

Another good example of a leveraged productivity credit union is the recent bill proposed by Representative Ellen Tauscher from California. The bill talks in terms of school infrastructure banks.

The issue is one of how to finance badly needed school construction in many places in the United States. Conservatives tend to favor leaving the matter to local school districts on the grounds that local people know best what their schools need. Liberals tend to favor federal aid for school construction on the grounds that only the federal government has the money to cover the costs.

The Tauscher bill achieves both the conservative goals and the liberal goals quite well, but without using (1) the conservative alternative, (2) the liberal alternative, or (3) a compromise alternative. A compromise would be that half the cost is covered locally, and half the cost is covered by the federal government.

The Tauscher bill provides that the federal government gives away no money for school construction in this context. It just loans money to a special bank. Maybe it loans $500,000. The bank then uses that $500,000 to borrow ten times the collateral from various places. The leveraged money is then available for school construction.

The Tauscher bill refers to these credit institutions as school infrastructure banks. The term leveraged productivity credit union is more descriptive and generic. It also builds on the more favorable connotation of a credit union, rather than a bank.

The borrowed money would be paid back by the state, local, and private institutions that are seeking to build new schools. This is like paying back the HUD money in the case of the United Farm Workers out of the rents, mortgage payments, and sales to the farm workers. Ellen Tauscher anticipates that in five years $2.5 billion in school construction loans and school construction could be paid off in this way.

Thus the leveraged productivity credit union or bank does have considerable potential for financing a variety of governmental and quasi-governmental activities without requiring a federal handout or gift and without unrealistically assuming that it can all be done locally. Like win-win performance pay, contracting out, vouchers, and competition, there may be a worthwhile future for win-win leveraged productivity credit unions.

Chapter 18

CREATIVE LEGISLATION IN THE U.S. IN THE 1900S

The purpose of this article is to pick a top dozen regarding federal legislation in the 1900s. Then ask what they tend to have in common that might explain these public policy innovations. By top ten, we mean congressional legislation that most historians would consider reasonably momentous in American political history. Momentous refers to congressional debate, impact, and relevant literature.

I. THE TOP DOZEN CONGRESSIONAL STATUTES

A. Economic Policy

1. Unemployment and inflation. Establishment of the Federal Reserve System.
2. Consumer policy in creating anti-trust and FTC. In the economic field, the Sherman and Clayton anti-trusts act. Federal Trade Commission and Pure Food and Drug Act.
3. Labor policy including NLRA. The Wagner Act or National Labor Relation Act, along with the Taft-Hartley amendments and fair labor standards.

B. Social Policy

4. Poverty including social security in the 1930s, but key court decisions in the 1960s. That recognizes that policy can come from the president like Keynsian policy, and from the courts, like poverty policy. Social Security, which covers a lot of subprograms regarding children, the blind, the disabled, and the aged.

5. Civil rights. The Civil Rights Statutes, especially 1964 on Fair Employment, also 1965 on Voting Rights, 1968 on Housing, 1957 and 1963 on Education. We could divide merit treatment into two, the legislation referred to above is civil rights legislation that relates to ethnic and gender discrimination. We could have a category that deals with other kinds of discrimination. Then, we would talk about the ADA which is the disability legislation. We would also talk about the anti-age discrimination. We could talk about hate crimes, but that is a state legislation.

C. Technology Policy

6. Environment. The legislation of the early 1970s under Nixon regarding air and water, and solid waste under Reagan.
7. Health policy, which includes Medicaid and Medicare. One could include the Clinton HMO program, but it did not pass. Before Medicaid and Medicare, we had Hill Burton money for hospitals provided that they serve the poor.
8. If we are going to say something about energy, we should definitely include as a monumental piece of legislation the 1996 legislation that provides for deregulation of the sale of electricity and communications. We could talk about the deregulation and competition-promoting legislation in general. That would include deregulation for the airlines and deregulation of interstate commerce. Some of that deregulation occurred under Reagan with regard to transportation. With regard to electricity and communications, it had been under Clinton.

D. Political Policy

9. Free Speech and civil liberties. That is the Supreme Court, not Congress or the President. However, the Internet of 2000 is a great free speech facilitator. Congress deserves no credit for that, they tried to interrupt with censorship legislation.
10. Motor voter registration.

E. International Policy

11. World peace. Here we could mention the Marshall plan. We could mention the Peace Corps and AID programs. Much of what has come out of the federal government with regard to world peace from 1945 to about 1995 has been Cold War activities which have resulted in

numerous wars throughout the world, not peace, including Vietnam, Korea, Central America, Central Africa, and Central Asia. It is disproportionately the central part of developing regions that are most impoverished and isolated, most subject to manipulation, and also where Americans have the least respect for human life. This is well illustrated with Guatemala, Nicaguara, and El Salvador in Latin America. Well illustrated with the Congo, South Africa, Ethiopia, and Yuganda in Africa. Also Mosambeek, Angloia, Ruwanda, and Burawandi. These are the American killing fields. Far worse than anything in Cambodia. For Asia, it is Cambodia, Laos, Vietnam, Afghanistan, Iraq, and Iran. Not much can honestly be said for American Peace policy in the 20th century. Or at least the second half of it. Government reform. That is partly a Supreme Court area with regard to the redistricting of state legislatures.

12. International trade including NAFTA, LATT, China trade, and tariff reduction for Africa and poor countries. The Clinton Free Trade Statutes like NAFTA, GATT, and maybe the new legislation dropping tariffs involving imports from poor countries in Africa and elsewhere.

II. Types of Policy Innovation

Did these occur during a democratic or republican administration? I can predict that under the Democrats the innovation probably favors the minorities. If under Republicans, the innovation probably favors business and well-to-do people.

Did the innovation occur during a time of war, depression, or prosperity? If during a time of war, I would predict that there would be nothing there, meaning no innovations. If in a time of depression, the innovations would be some anti-depressing activity. That does not give much predictably. We have only had one depression in the twentieth century. We may never have another one. Prosperity is good for innovation, which actually runs contrary to some common sense. One would think that in bad times people would welcome change. The opposite may be true. In bad times, people are filled with anxieties. They certainly cannot tolerate change very well if it means increased rights for women, minorities, or labor. The can maybe tolerate change for consumers because everyone is a consumer.

Prosperity is also important because many of these programs cost money, and it helps to have more revenue coming in to the federal government than expense. That may not be true. Under traditional recession-fighting economics, the government is supposed to do its big spending when times are sort of bad in order to pump money into the economy. Most of these programs do not cost big money anyhow. There is no big money involved in prohibiting discrimination on the basis of race or gender.

These innovations can definitely be classified by substance. That helps think of what the innovations might be. Substance includes economic, technology, social, political, international, and legal.

III. Causes of Creative Legislation

Possible explanations for why these legislative innovations occurred when they did might include the following:

1. Political Parties
2. Personalities
3. Crisis Situations
4. Social Forces, Movements, and Interest Groups
5. Political and Social Science

There are partisan factors observable. Nearly all the examples occurred during Democratic administrations. The Democrats are more in favor of change and innovation. Environmental protection is more a middle class activity than the others. Likewise, deregulation tends to be a pro-business activity for businesses that want to enter into the market to buy products.

Not all Democrats as presidents are equally innovative. The key presidents were Wilson, Roosevelt, Kennedy-Johnson, and Clinton. There is nothing very innovative about the other Democrats, although there have not been very many others in the twentieth century. The others include Truman and Carter. Just two. We cannot do much generalizing from that small of a sample. We could say that presidents that serve two terms have more of an opportunity to do good legislation. The causal direction may be the opposite. That means that doing good legislation gets them re-elected.

One can argue that crisis situations provoke the legislation and who happens to be president is irrelevant. That seems to be untrue if the biggest crisis we have had in the twentieth century have been wars. World War I, World War II, the Korean War, the Vietnam War, and the Cold War stimulated no creativity. They stifled creativity. The depression may have stimulated some creativity with regard to labor legislation and social security, but that is only two of the ten.

One can think in terms of social forces as part of a kind of historical dialectic, going into the start of the twentieth century or going back to the start of the nineteenth century. The landed aristocrats controlled U.S. and Western Europe. The new merchant class rose up partly through factory technology and trading technology with regard to transportation. They overthrew the landed aristocrats in the French Revolution, the American Revolution, but that does not mean legislation. It means the U.S. Constitution and the Bill of Rights and the French Constitution. Nothing much happened, though, until the end of the 1900s, especially the beginning of the twentieth century in the U.S. when labor rose up against factory managers and owners and established labor legislation in the 1930s in the U.S. Before that, consumers in effect rose up and established pro-consumer legislation under Woodrow Wilson. Then in the 1960s, minorities and women rose up and established civil rights legislation. In the 1970s there was an environmental movement. In the 1980s, a deregulation movement. In the 1990s, a free trade movement. What all these have in common is the need for a large influential block of people to object to existing conditions and to push or demand for remedial legislation.

Since our audience is academics, disproportionately, we should say something about the role of academics:

Woodrow Wilson had a Ph.D. in political science and was a professor of public administration at Princeton. Then he was president of Princeton.

FDR had a brain trust that included especially Charles Merriam from the political science department at the University of Chicago who is considered one of the founders of modern political science.

We then move up to the Kennedy-Johnson period. Especially Kennedy, but also Johnson. The leading description of the Kennedy administration is by Halberstam. The book is entitled The Best and the Brightest. It emphasizes all the academic types. As for political scientists, the closest name that stands out is Arthur Slusinger, a historian. One should note that FDR had lots of law professors like Felix Frankfurter before he was appointed to the Supreme Court.

IV. SOME REFERENCES

An interesting book on creative legislation is Nelson Polsby, *Political Innovation in America: The Politics of Policy Initiation* (Yale, 1984). This book deals with eight legislative case studies on which information could be readily obtained, rather than eight or a dozen examples of highly important or creative legislation. To some extent, the Polsby book illustrates social science research that focuses on less important units of analysis where the light is good, rather than on key units where information is not so readily available.

He finds that the underlying causes are having an innovation-prone culture and having needs. The U.S. may be an innovative culture on technology matters, but it has not been so innovative on public policy. Almost all 12 of the above examples of creative legislation were adopted in earlier years by countries in Western Europe. The U.S. may lag behind on egalitarian policies because immigration tends to push people up without requiring public policy to do so. Saying that the second most important factor is need is like the cliché that necessity is the mother of invention. What we are concerned with is not so much why public policies have been adopted, but why they get adopted when they do. Since the need may long precede the adoption, and the adoption stays after the need is past.

Other relevant books include the literature that deals with agenda setting and policy formulation. That literature does talk about what causes or triggers the process of creative legislation. The literature includes:

1. James Anderson, *Public Policy Making: An Introduction* (Houghton Mifflin, 1997),
2. Christopher Basso, "The Practice and Study of Policy Formation" in S. Nagel (ed.), *Encyclopedia of Policy Studies* (Marcel Dekker, 1994).

3. Garry Brewer and Peter DeLeon, *The Foundations of Policy Analysis* (Dorsey Press, 1983).
4. Robert Eyestone (ed.), *Public Policy Formation* (JAI Press, 1984).
5. Larry Gertson, *Public Policy Making: Process and Principles* (M.E. Sharpe, 1997).
6. Charles Jones, *An Introduction to the Study of Public Policy*, (Brooks/Cole, 1984).
7. John Kingdon, *Agendas, Alternatives, and Public Policies* (Little, Brown, 1984).

Chapter 19

CREATIVITY AND EXTREMISM

The purpose of this short article is to discuss what role the extreme left and the extreme right play in developing new and useful public policies.

On the relation between extremism and creativity. Extremists definitely tend to come up with novel ideas. That is why they are called extremists. As to whether they are useful ideas. That is unlikely in a democracy. At least it is unlikely in the intermediate or the long run. Because any constructive ideas get co-opted by the mainstream parties.

We mentioned in the PE news for Autumn that the Republicans are good for getting left-wing ideas adopted, and the Democrats are good for getting right-wing ideas adopted. The Democrats think up the left wing ideas, but they cannot get them adopted without Republican help, and vice versa. That's mainstream creativity, not extremist. Creativity and implementation.

I. IN GENERAL

A. The Extreme Left: Co-Opting

The general conclusion for which we will give examples is that the extreme left does develop new and useful ideas such as the 10 points in the Communist Manifesto or the 1932 platform of the U.S. Communist Party, but those useful ideas quickly get co-opted by mainstream liberals and even conservatives. The extremist parties and interest groups in democracies then tend to disappear or to drastically change what they advocate.

B. The Extreme Right: Rejecting

As for the extreme right, they develop novel ideas (even bizarre ones) on subjects like racism, sexism, class bias, imperialism, and dictatorship. Those right-wing interest groups, however, also have to drastically change but not because their ideas get co-opted. Instead they change because they are advocating things that are so contrary to long-term historical trends since the Renaissance (virtually ending medievalism), the French Revolution (virtually ending absolute monarchies), and the end of Nazism in World War II (virtually ending extreme racism, imperialism, and dictatorship).

II. THE 1930S AND BEFORE

A. The Extreme Left: New and Sometimes Useful

Give the 10 points from the Communist Manifesto. That means xeroxing some pages out of the PPG book, which may have already appeared in the PE news, but this is for the Creativity Plus news. And it is altogether different context. This is on creativity, not on policy versus private sector. The key pages are 185. More specifically see pages 198-201. It would be good if we get a copy of the platform of the Communist party of 1932. Put a note into the Internet file to see if it is obtainable. We should be able to get a copy out of the library. The important thing is to know that the Communist party advocated social security as a key plank. The Democrats and Republicans opposed social security. The Communists also advocated minimum wages, maximum hours, no child labor, safe work places, no Jim Crow, unions.

In examining trends from 1850 to 1950, one is struck by how much of what was considered socialistic in 1850 has been accepted without controversy in the United States since 1950. A dramatic illustration is to note the ten points Karl Marx advocated in the Communist Manifesto of 1848 and the extent to which they are now part of American government and economy:

1. "Abolition of property in land and application of all rents of land to public purposes." People can still own land, but we now have zoning laws, building codes, and rent control.
2. "A heavy progressive or graduated income tax." Income taxes are now the main source of revenue for the American government.
3. "Abolition of all right of inheritance." People still inherit, but there are federal and state inheritance and estate taxes.
4. "Confiscation of property of all emigrants and rebels." The United States has had no violent socialist revolution in which that might have occurred. The property of emigrants was often confiscated after the American Revolution, and so was the property of southern rebels after the Civil War.
5. "Centralization of credit in the hands of the State." We have had a Bank of the United States since the early 1800's and a Federal Reserve System since the early 1900's.

6. "Centralization of the means of communication and transport in the hands of the State." We have had agencies regulating interstate communication, interstate commerce, civil aeronautics, and maritime shipping for some time. Now the government owns passenger railroads, municipal transportation, airports, and highways.
7. "Extension of factories and instruments of production owned by the state." The Tennessee Valley Authority and municipal utilities are an example of that.
8. "Equal liability of all to labor." Wartime and peacetime conscription exemplifies this point as do the work-incentive rules for public aid.
9. "Combination of agriculture with manufacturing." The United States has long had industrialized agriculture, with farms now more accessible
10. "Free education and abolition of children's factory labor." The United States pioneered free public schools and state universities. Child labor has been illegal nationwide since the 1930's.

B. The Extreme Right: New And Disfunctional

We need to get a comparable copy of the Nazi party platform as of 1932. It has to be the same year. 1932 was also a good year because it was like a time of blank slate for public policy. In which people were rejecting the previous conventional wisdom about public policy. They were ready for new ideas. They accepted the Communist ones through the Democratic party. "They" rejected the Nazi ones. "They" even included the Republican party. On the right, they seem to never come up with any constructive useful ideas. They do come up with novel ideas. New in the sense of hair-brained bizarre. But not useful. The changing world times works too much against the right wing extremist coming up with anything that is likely to be adopted. They advocate ideas that have to do with five key topics. All of which run contrary to long term trends, at least since the Renaissance:

1. *Racism*, sexism, and other ways of discriminating against people, other than merit treatment. Racism and non-merit treatment are also out because conservative business interests want to hire on the basis of merit. The workers object to being displaced by women and minorities. Business does the displacing.
2. Justifying poverty and the idea that poor people are at fault for their own poverty. A kind of survival of the fittest. Poor people practically by definition being unfit. The *capitalistic* element comes in the class conflict item by siding with the haves against the have-nots. Also on the matter of class conflict. Business as of 2000 is not concerned with whether poor people are the cause of poverty. Business wants to see poor people become better customers and less of a drain on the tax payer. Business is concerned with the remedies for poverty, not the

causes. The remedies relate to economic growth, training, placement, transportation subsidies.

3. An attitude of *imperialism* toward the world. This clearly is out as of the year 2000 when big business does not want to go to war. To conquer territory. It wants to obtain customers sources, supply, investment outlets, investment money, all of which require world peace and prosperity.

4. A fourth right wing extremist idea is *dictatorship*. That seems to be out. It is not enough just to say that there is a worldwide trend toward more voter choice. More voter participation, two party systems, multiple party systems. We have to say why this is so. It is so because on all of these points, one could say the left has threatened and demanded. More important though may be the fact that the moderate right meaning the business right recognizes that it may be in their own best interest to support modern versions of all of these. Worldwide democracy leads to better decision making with regard to peace and prosperity. Which is good for American sales. Democracy is profitable. Especially on a cross-national basis. Domestically, the right is not so much in favor of some aspects of democracy like easier registration in voting. The ideologist recognized that a free market for business products is closely related ideologically to a free market place for ideas. Thus the libertarian right endorses the free speech aspects of Democracy.

III. SINCE THE 1930S

We could update 1932, but nothing new has been recommended by Communism or Nazism since 1932. The American Communist party hasn't had a new idea since 1932 that wasn't co-opted by the Democrats. In the 1930s it dealt with economic policy. The Communists deserve no credit for race and gender ideas which the Democrats adopted in the 1960s. On race, the Communist Party recommended carving out a state such as Mississippi for blacks to live in sort of like Liberia in the United States or like the Jewish province in Eastern Siberia under Stalin. No co-opting of that. On sexism, the Communist Party until maybe 1970 took the position that women were both a sexual distraction and an ideological distraction. If we just got rid of capitalism, discrimination against blacks and women would also disappear. There are variations on socialism in East Europe with plenty of discrimination still present. The women factor is largely technological. The race factor and both are largely matters of capitalist employers deciding that they are willing to hire competent people regardless of gender and race, and also deciding that they want to appeal to those people to buy their products.

Chapter 20

THE CREATIVITY OF REVOLUTIONARIES

In the recent issue of the MKM News we have a mural that analyzes modern revolutions. It talks about five revolutions.

I. THE REVOLUTIONS

A. Anti-Colonial

The first set of revolutions lasted from 1776 to about 1810. It covered all of North and South America. Every single country revolted against colonial oppression from Europe except Canada. Canada did revolt too, but it was unsuccessful. Haiti revolted from France. From Mexico to Argentina, Bolivar freed all the countries from Spain. The U.S. revolted form England. That left a few British colonies. France in the Caribbean had nobody living in them except Native Americans, meaning Indians and some slaves. Although, slaves conducted the successful revolt in Haiti. All of those Caribbean colonies did gain their independence but not until about the 1960s, meaning about 150 years later, in the case of Barbados, Jamaica, Trinidad, British Guyana, Dutch Surinam, French Guyana is still French Guyana. The explanation might be that French colonies were always run so rotten that nobody wanted to move to them, thus nobody lives in French Guyana who wants to revolt against France. It is a jungle, literally unlike British Guyana which has a high degree of civilization. British Guyana attracted lots of people from India and Pakistan. French Guyana attracted none even though it's the same climate and geography.

The other wave of revolutions to establish sovereignty did not occur until 150 years later, meaning simultaneously with the Barbados revolution. People don't think of Barbados as having a revolution, and it did not really have one. It just suddenly found one day that the British had gone. Possibly gone to India where there was a real revolution or possibly just gone back to London. Or to a considerable extent gone back into their fancy houses in Barbados. Elsewhere in the British Empire there was violent/semi-violent revolution throughout Africa and Asia, all of which was successful. Every former British colony broke free although not all at once. The first in Africa was Kenya in 1960, and the last was South Africa in 1990. All of those revolutions, whether they were the U.S. in 1776, or South Africa in 1990 involve some pretty creative people such as Mandela of South Africa. That refutes the idea that a social revolution involves a different kind of revolutionary than a political revolution. South Africa was more a social revolution with oppressed blacks getting their voting rights from oppressive whites. South Africa was not revolting against Britain or Holland. Holland was thrown out in the Boer War almost a 100 years before that. Britain was thrown out in about 1950 by the Afrikaans not the blacks. There was an element of indigenous people vs. foreigners. South Africa was a combination of class conflict and international cultural conflict.

The U.S. had much more international conflict but not cultural, and not especially class either. There is nothing in the Bill of Rights even about merit treatment, just the opposite. The U.S. Constitution condones slavery which is the worst kind of class system, worse than even the caste system in India. The U.S. deserves no credit in those years for contributing to treating people as equals regardless what the Declaration of Independence says. One could say the Declaration of Independence is the height of utter hypocrisy. It's not really at least in part because one can say that Jefferson who wrote it did feel a bit ambivalent about slavery and was going to include a paragraph on it but was overruled by a majority of the revolutionary congress.

B. Economic Class

Looking back at our list of revolutions, they divide into two. Those that are anti-colonial to establish a sovereign state either in the Western or Eastern hemisphere. The second category is a revolution to change the class system. That's the French revolution, overthrowing medieval feudalism and replacing it with a kind of bourgeois capitalism. The French revolutionaries were not Marxists, pro-labor, as there was no significant proletariat class as of 1789.

The next wave of revolutions though did involve workers at the barricades in 1848. That's a big year for revolutions in Ireland and Germany that sound unrelated. People think of the Irish revolution as having something to do with the potato famine and the German revolution with having something to do with Prussians trying to take over and instilling their more authoritarian thinking on the more democratic thinking of the West Germans who were influenced by Napoleonic France. That sounds like two different causes. The reality though is as of 1850 West Europe was undergoing tremendous turmoil because the industrial revolution which is associated with the capitalistic revolution was creating factories that were filthy, used child labor, and exploited people who used to live on farms in healthy environments. That was true in France, Germany, Scandinavia, Italy, Poland, Dublin, Belfast, not in rural areas. The rural people moved to the cities because they were no longer so needed on their farms due to mechanization and sometimes due to fencing that forced them off. They were a variation on squatters without an actual title. They then moved to the cities where their wives and children were subject to economic exploitation and they revolted. The potato famine helped because it drove farmers off the farms. It would have been much worse but both Ireland and Germany had the safety valve of going to the U.S. 1848 was a big year for Irish and German immigration to America.

The next wave of revolutions was the early 1900s. It helps to see the big picture. People who are narrowly focused think maybe only in terms of the 1917 revolution in Russia. It was an important revolution. But related revolutions were occurring in Mexico that involved overthrowing a feudalistic culture but skipping over partly the capitalistic country just like they did in Russia and moving towards a more socialistic culture. This was partly true in other Latin American countries but maybe not until the Depression years of the 1930s. It was certainly true in countries in Western Europe where socialist parties became very important after WWI in England, France, and Scandinavia. They became important without violence but they were still revolutionary with regard to what they advocated and what they achieved, especially after WWII. One can definitely have a revolution without violence when there is a big change in the constitution of a country and especially the rules governing relations between the government and the private sector.

Those two revolutions could be lumped together as economic class revolutions. One involves replacing feudalism with capitalism and the other involves replacing capitalism with variations on socialism. Thus we have two kinds of revolution, nation-state revolutions and economic class revolutions.

C. Democracy Revolutions

The third kind are democracy revolutions. That's the newest. That's what happened at Tiananmen square in 1989 in China, and what happened in Thailand in 1992 when the military government was replaced with a civilian government. That's what happened with Gorbachev in the Soviet Union, especially his glasnost policy which is more important in the history of Russia than selling out or giving away some state-owned farms or factories. Democracy in Russia meant the end of a one-party system. The one-party system also ended in all the other Eastern European countries and many of the African and Latin American countries at about the same time. In Latin America it was the end of the Fascist Party rather than the Communist Party in Argentina, Chile, Uruguay, Paraguay, Brazil, all of Central America. In Africa, one-party systems were overthrown that were neither Communist nor Fascist, but personallismo systems where the one party was built around some individual who was a dictator such as Malawi, Zambia, Uganda, and countries that are still trying to get rid of their dictators like current Kenya. Also, the semi-ideological dictatorship in Ethiopia. Definitely Zaire, which is now the Congo, which was a non-ideological dictatorship under Mobuto.

II. THE CREATIVITY

Each of these revolutions had creative people.

A. Anti-Colonial

The American Revolution had some highly creative people like Jefferson, Madison, Hamilton who wrote the Federalist Papers together and separately. They also wrote the Declaration of Independence and the Constitution. At the same time as the American Revolution, there were creative leaders elsewhere in the WESTERN HEMISPHERE, although what they wrote is not so well-known, such as Simon Bolivar, Toussaint Leovture, and the hero of the Mexican Revolution. Mexico has a separate revolutionary hero because they never really got their sovereign independence until about the time of the American Civil War. The French invaded Mexico while the Civil War was going on. The U.S. fought the Mexican-American War against Mexico and took away half of Mexico. Juarez is the name of the Mexican Revolutionary, but that may have been the second Mexican Revolution, which was mainly directed against France. The first revolution directed against Spain involved Simon Bolivar as the hero even though he may have never come to Mexico. He got Spain to withdraw from all of Latin America, including countries that did not physically revolt. With the exception of Cuba and Puerto Rico, which the U.S. took away in 1898. Looking in Magruder's textbook at page 85, the first Mexican revolutionary is Hidalgo from 1810, who was in effect the Simon Bolivar of Mexico. Juarez was 1857, and then in 1910, the leading names are Madera, Zapata, and Villa. And then in the depression years the leading name is Cardenas. Now it's Vicente Fox, who can be considered a revolutionary but more in the democratic sense than in the economic class conflict. He peacefully overthrew the one party system.

For thinkers in the fourth set of revolutions that involve nation-states in the EASTERN HEMISPHERE. Gandhi is the leader of non-violent passive revolution. One problem with his creativity though is a lack of books or writings. The previous people have all written something important that libraries have.

1. Jefferson was the top creative person of the American Revolution, author of Bill of Rights and Declaration of Independence.
2. John Locke has books and so does Rousseau.
3. Karl Marx certainly has books like *Das Capital* and the *Communist Manifesto*.
4. People write about Gandhi and passive resistance and they certainly talk about it, Martin Luther King talked about it a lot. The Gandhi movie though does not show Gandhi to be an author. The only bibliographic references in the Magruder book to Gandhi are either biography book or autobiography, rather than books communicating his philosophy. The 1932 book called *His Own Story* may communicate his philosophy but

that was 15 years before he died and his philosophy may have changed or been added to.

B. Economic Class

Creative people in the capitalist revolution that OVERTHREW FEUDALISM would include all those British thinkers like John Locke, and Thomas Hobbes, although he was more sympathetic to feudalism. We don't need to see how many names we can come up with. Locke is the leading British revolutionary thinker and Rousseau is the leading French one. Voltaire was too many years ahead of the French Revolution, not in the sense of being premature but just not being a contemporary.

Creative people in the SOCIALIST REVOLUTION include Karl Marx who so dominates the thinking that it's almost hard to come up with someone else. In Russia, Leon Trotsky. In Germany, maybe Rosa Luxembourg. She was the leader and a leading thinker with regard to revolutionary Marxism at the time of the Weimar Republic. Other socialist thinkers at the time tended to be revisionists such as Burnstein, whose creativity is questionable. They were can't-do thinkers. Being a can't do thinker is contrary to being creative. I'm not sure about Rosa Luxembourg's creativity. She is a little more like Robespierre meaning a barricades fighter than like Marx meaning a person who haunts the British library.

C. Democracy Revolutions

For the fifth set of revolutions which relate to MODERN DEMOCRACY, the leading people are Gorbachev, who doesn't write something that's considered a great work of ideas. This leads us to say that revolutionaries consist of thinkers and doers and usually not both together. Gandhi was more a doer than a thinker, so is Gorbachev. Locke and Rousseau are thinkers. Washington was a doer but didn't do much thinking. He never wrote anything I'm aware of. Jefferson was definitely a thinker but he never was a minuteman, he was not a Mel Gibson. Jefferson was never known to throw a tomahawk at anyone.

D. Win-Win Thinking

One revolution that we did not make very explicit is the CURRENT GLOBALISM REVOLUTION that involves free trade, economic growth and lifetime learning. The heroes of that revolution include:

1. Bill Clinton definitely deserves some credit for free trade association with NAFTA and GATT, also tremendous economic growth in the U.S.

which has affected the world by way of providing an atmosphere that is conducive to business development.

2.   The globalism revolution also can consider FDR as a doer being the key person responsible for the United Nations and Woodrow Wilson with his responsibility for the League of Nations.

3.   Also very important is Mr. Schumann, who founded the European Union. These people are all doers, not much in the way of writers.

4.   In our mural above the SOS door, we also include Hugo Grotius as a hero of globalism. He did do a lot of writing but long ago and maybe somewhat narrow. He is a key author of ideas on international law. Globalism though means more international economics than law. What law there is in globalism is business law, not public international law that deals with treaties and the rules of war. Business law means how do you enforce a contract between a U.S. seller and a Chinese buyer, or vice versa. That was not Hugo Grotius. It was maybe more William Blackstone, who wrote on British Common Law, which has now been elevated to international common law, or an international code of commercial law.

We have a sixth set of revolutions that have not yet occurred. They involve a kind of WIN-WIN COMPOSITE of what is referred to as the best of capitalism, socialism, and democracy. That could be definitely considered a revolution even though it doesn't involve any violence. Win-win analysis is a revolutionary way of thinking as contrasted to compromise or win-lose. If this is going to come about in the next generation, it's not going to have doers who man the barricades since there are no barricades. It could involve a U.S. president who campaigns on a win-win platform. He/she would be a doer, maybe Hillary Clinton, even if they don't write any books on the subject. We are working on writing some books on the subject. But it's only in an infancy stage. Although catching on as indicated as by our numerous win-win mentions.

III. DOERS AND THINKERS

It is relevant to talk about what kinds of revolutions there are. However, we do not have a different kind of creativity for each kind of revolution. Instead we have classified revolutionary leaders as DOERS AND THINKERS. The thinkers are creative in the sense that they create books and other materials like the Communist Manifesto which is just a pamphlet or the Declaration of Independence which is two pages. The Bill of Rights can fit on one page. The doers bring about revolutions. Or they help administer them by being an elected president or being in charge of some kind of brigade. The classic doer-thinker combination might be Washington and Jefferson, or Napoleon and Rousseau. Trotsky was unusual in that he to some extent was the Washington and the Jefferson of the Russian Revolution. Lenin was also the

Washington and the Jefferson. They both wrote books and also had leadership positions. Even Stalin did both but with evil goals, whereas Trotsky's goals were more democratic. Lenin is more ambiguous, he died before he had a chance to clarify his goals.

Chapter 21

INNOVATION VERSUS DIFFUSION

When I talk on win-win policy analysis in developing nations, some of the participants express concern that the ideas are not applicable to developing nations or their specific developing nation because they lack sufficient technological skills or sufficient financial resources.

I. WHEN TECHNOLOGY AND ECONOMICS ARE HURDLES

Lack of technology or technological feasibility can sometimes be a problem in win-win implementation. For example one can easily say that the win-win solution to satisfying profit-oriented conservatives and clean-environment liberals is to develop new technologies that will be both more profitable and cleaner. This has been done in such areas as processing soybeans, panning for gold, and finding replacements for aerosol propellants. We have not, however, found a technology that will enable us to speed up the half-life of nuclear waste so that waste turns into lead within a day or a week, rather than only after hundreds of years. Physicists even disagree as to whether it is chemically or economically possible. This is an important example where technology is presently a surmountable hurdle at best or an impossible obstacle at worst.

Lack of financial resources can also sometimes be a problem in win-win implementation. For example one can easily say that solar energy is both cleaner and less expensive than fossil-fuel energy. This is true in frying an egg with a magnifying glass that focuses the sun on the bottom of a bowl of water in which the egg is placed. It may also be true of solar panes on top of a house to supplement the furnace in the wintertime. We do know the technology for putting a microwave into the sky which will be the equivalent of a worldwide magnifying glass or solar pane. This microwave can be engineered to tilt toward different parts of the earth's surface every second over a 24-hour period so every part of the earth's surface gets lots of solar energy for running factories and lighting cities, not just frying eggs or providing extra winter heat to houses. The economic cost of such a microwave in the sky presently is trillions of dollars more than the world can afford. This is presently a true economic hurdle or obstacle.

II. THE FALSITY OF THE TECHNOLOGY EXCUSE

These problems, however, are quite different from what people in developing nations are generally talking about when they refer to technological and economic obstacles. The big difference is that what is considered a technological or economic obstacle may be quite manageable. This may even be true for an impoverished nation where most of the people earn less than $1 a day and where most of the people cannot read or write. The reason these problems are generally manageable is because we are talking about the diffusion of new technologies or new policies, not the innovation or invention of them. It may take Thomas Edison and a Menlo Park laboratory to invent a light bulb, but any two-year-old child in a developing or industrial nation can turn on a light switch that operates through a wire attached to a community generator.

A good example of the falsity of the technological excuse for adopting new technologies is the widespread polio in Malawi prior to about 1990. I was in Malawi in 1987 as a USIA speaker. I was given a Fight Polio pin by a government official. That night, when I spoke before the Malawi Bar Association, a lawyer said I see you have been co-opted by the government into thinking we have polio in Malawi because we are a low-technology nation. The lawyers argued that the Salk and Sabin polio vaccines had long ago been invented. In fact long enough that the 17-year patent had run out, and the vaccine could be made in massive quantities without paying royalties. Better yet, it could be obtained without charge from the United Nations or donor countries. It could then be put into paper cups and administered to children in the villages by any adult. That includes adults who can not read or write, but who can pour vaccine into a paper cup and hand it to a child to drink.

This would be a win-win solution in the sense that it would improve the health and the quality of life of Malawi children. It would relieve the anxieties and burdens on their parents. It would mean lower public health costs for the nation. The government could get credit for having saved children's lives, which is generally worth lots of votes. The donor countries could rightfully feel good about this kind of aid to developing nations.

If there is no technological or economic obstacle, and there are such great win-win benefits, then why weren't polio vaccines administered in Malawi to any significant extent before 1990? The answer according to the lawyers of the Malawi Bar Association is dictatorship and a lack of free speech. By that they are referring to Hastings Kazuma Banda, the pre-1990 Malawi President for Life. He insisted that only doctors or nurses could administer polio vaccine even in liquid cup form. Lawyers who objected to that policy as being irrational ran the risk of being suspended from practice. If they objected too strongly or too broadly, they ran the risk of imprisonment and even possible execution. When Hastings Banda was overthrown by the people and at least a minimum level of free speech was re-established, then lay administration of polio vaccine won out in the marketplace of ideas on how to deal with that highly serious health policy problem.

III. THE FALSITY OF THE ECONOMICS EXCUSE

Adult training is another good example which emphasizes alleged economic obstacles to the transmission of innovative practices. When I was in Namibia in 1999 talking about win-win economic development, I mentioned that President Clinton in his State of the Union speech had advocated giving training vouchers to every adult American in order to raise the skill levels of the labor force in a decentralized way. The Namibians rightly said they could not afford Clinton's proposal of a $2000 voucher per person. My response was to ask whether they could afford $100 per person. Their response to that was that they could afford $100 per person, but it would not buy much in the way of training.

My response was twofold. First it is amazing how the private sector market can come forth to get vouchers out of people by offering them the specified products or services. I saw that in Mississippi in 1967 when welfare recipients had a $10 a month housing allowance and landlords provided shacks for $10 a month to get the $10 vouchers. Second it is amazing how the potential trainee will scrounge to match the $100 or to come up with some of his own funds if the computer literacy course or truck driving course that he wants costs $150. That is especially likely to occur if the voucher clearly says on it that it can only be used for training, and it further says that studies have shown that a small amount of money invested in training can result in an additional $10,000, $100,000 or $1,000,000 in lifetime earnings depending on whether one is in Namibia, the United States, or somewhere in between.

Their response to that was to raise the obstacle or hurdle of administrative feasibility by saying the private sector trainers would cheat the trainees or sometimes they would be in cahoots to cash in the government voucher and spend the money. My response to that was the voucher can specify on its face that the trainer can not cash in the voucher unless the trainee passes a test showing the trainee has newly achieved the qualifications of being computer literate, being able to drive a truck, or whatever the training is designed to achieve. The trainee is not likely to give half the value of the voucher to a crooked trainer since the trainee thereby loses the incremental $10,000 in lifetime earnings which the crooked trainer is not likely to give him. The voucher can also specify that the trainer gets double the value of the voucher if the trainee is placed in a new job or position for at least six months.

Their at-first skeptical responses also said this is not possible for Namibia because it doesn't have the university system for doing the training which is a variation on not being high tech. Just as it is amazing how business firms will adjust their prices to fit the vouchers that they are seeking to cash in, they will also create and adjust their training courses. Thus if the Namibians want truck driving, computer literacy, or some other skill frequently offered at the high school level, then training firms will spring up in light of those profit making opportunities.

Other skeptics will say the potential trainers do not know what training they will need. This is the individual psychology hurdle. The easy and accurate response is that they know what they need better than anyone else does. They roughly know what their abilities are, what their interests are, and what jobs are available. The potential trainers will also test the trainees for ability, interests, and job availability because the trainers do not get paid unless the trainee passes a qualifying credentializing test, and the trainers don't get paid as much unless they can place the trainee in a job for at least six months. Also, the competition among trainers and the word of mouth plus published advertising will filter out the bad trainers and generate more customers for the good trainers.

The bottom line of this example is that Namibia may be able to adopt this win-win solution to training more easily than the high tech United States. It is a win-win because it provides a decentralized capitalistic approach to a policy problem that should please conservatives. It also provides a form of universal training for low income adults and others which can lead to higher lifetime earnings which should please liberals. Both conservatives and liberals should be pleased by the wonders that this can do for economic growth.

IV. THE POLITICAL HURDLE

In light of all that why has it not been adopted in the United States? The answer is probably the political feasibility obstacle. The Democrat Clinton proposed the idea in his 1998 State of the Union speech to a rather partisan Republican Congress that had just come through bitter impeachment proceedings. They were reluctant to adopt anything that Clinton proposed no matter how good it might be for the economy including using the budget surplus to greatly lower the national debt and thereby greatly lower the interest rates charged to business. Namibia does not have that kind of political feasibility hurdle.

In fact, it might be noted that Namibia seems to have invented the system of greatly increasing voter participation while not allowing double voting. Namibia with a low technology and little money developed the idea of having voters put their right hand into a bowl of lemon juice. The lemon juice is invisible unless it is put under a light bulb that is ultraviolet or infrared, costing maybe less than $1 a light bulb. That way Namibia can have on site registration, holiday voting, and voting at one's work precinct or home precinct which the United States does not have and not worry about double voting. Maybe the excuse of the United States is that it has not yet reached the light bulb technology or that it can not afford water and lemon juice. Maybe the real reason is also political feasibility, namely that incumbent politicians do not want a lot of new voters who might vote them out of office, or worse a lot of low income voters who might change the allocation of things of value in society.

V. MORE EXAMPLES AND CONCLUSIONS

We could give lots more examples of the non-adoption of win-win solutions in developing nations on the alleged grounds of lack of technological feasibility, economic feasibility, administrative feasibility, or other excuses for inertia, skepticism, cynicism, or negativism. We could also give lots more examples of non-adoption of win-win solutions in industrial nations like the U.S. On knowingly phony excuses such as trainers and trainees are inherently corrupt and voters inherently want to vote multiple times. The important point is that people in general from both developing and industrial countries are often reluctant to adopt new ideas that they were not previously aware of and that they find embarrassing. The important sub-point for the purposes of this article in Creativity Plus is that it is or should be relatively and absolutely easy usually to adopt new ideas and even new technologies that have already been invented and developed elsewhere. Innovation may by definition require creativity, but transmission and diffusion should only require an open mind and positive thinking which emphasize how relatively easy hindsight and following the lead of what has already been shown by experience or reasoning to be quite manageable regardless of alleged hurdles to be overcome.

POSTSCRIPT

These ideas that transmission-diffusion is easier than innovation or creativity also apply to win-win analysis. There may be some creativity in originating win-win analysis or in originating some of the early solutions, but there have now been so many examples and typologies that one can quickly find win-win solutions to policy problems by reasoning by analogy from what has already been done. Numerous examples of that can be given from my experience in China where I mentioned types of win-win solutions, and graduate students in political science at the People's University raised their hands to say that is just like our agriculture, transportation, education, or other problem. See Nagel, *Creativity and Public Policy: Generating Super-Optimum Solutions* (Ashgate, 2000) and "Win-Win Foresight and Hindsight" in the Autumn 2000 issue of *Policy Evaluation*.

PART FOUR:

CREATIVITY BIBLIOGRAPHIES

Chapter 22

CREATIVITY BOOKS BY SUBJECTS

In the Autumn 1999 issue of Creativity Plus, we published an alphabetical list of books and articles on creativity. The articles in Creativity Plus since then have included useful references depending on the subjects of the articles. We would now like to present a bibliography consisting only of books (not articles) and with the books divided into six major subjects, rather than alphabetically, although alphabetically within each subject.

The subjects are (1) how-to-do-it creativity books, (2) books that deal with creativity from a social science perspective, especially psychology and sociology, (3) books that deal with creativity in business, private sector management, or not-for-profit organizations, (4) books on creativity in science and technology, (5) books on creativity in visual art, music, and literature, (6) books on creativity in developing public policies and the role of public policy in promoting creativity, and (7) books dealing with creativity in philosophy, theory, and religion. These subjects are most in accordance with the purpose of the *Creativity Plus* quarterly and the C+ Association. That purpose is to be usefully innovative in solving diverse problems, especially public policy problems.

The stars next to seven of the books indicate which book in each of the seven categories was considered by the C+ editors to be the best book in that category. If we were to recommend one overall best book, we would recommend the *Creativity Encyclopedia* edited by Mark Runco. It is almost a set of books in itself since it runs 1,693 pages. The C+ editors felt that *Creativity Plus* is the best journal in the field, although their opinion may have involved a conflict of interest.

I. CREATIVITY HOW-TO-DO-IT MANUALS

1. Tony Buzan, *Make the Most of Your Mind* (Linden Press/Simon-Schuster, 1984), 149 p.
2. Edward de Bono, *de Bono's Thinking Course* (Facts on File, 1994), 186 p.
3. Richard Fobes, *The Creative Problem Solver's Toolbox* (Solutions Through Innovation, 1993).
4. John Hayes, *The Complete Problem Solver* (Erlbaum, 1989), 375 p.
5. James Higgins, *Escape from the Maze: 9 Steps to Personal Creativity* (New Management, 1997), 250 p.
6. Fred Lichtgarn, *Basic Components of Creativity* (AIM Publications, 1979), 89 p.
7. Michael Michalko, *Cracking Creativity: The Secrets of Creative Genius* (Ten Speed Press, 1998), 309 p.
8. Robert and Michele Root-Bernstein, *Sparks of Genius* (Houghton Mifflin, 1999), 401 p.
9. Todd Siler, *Think Like A Genius* (Bantam Books, 1996), 294 p.
10. Mike Vance and Diane Deacon, *Break Out of the Box* (Career Press, 1996), 223 p.
11. Mike Vance and Diane Deacon, *Think Out of the Box* (Career Press, 1995), 216 p.

II. SOCIAL SCIENCE ANALYSIS OF CREATIVITY

1. James Austin, *Chase, Chance, and Creativity* (Columbia, 1978), 237 p.
2. Margaret Boden, *The Creative Mind: Myths & Mechanisms* (Basic Books, 1990), 303 p.
3. Howard Gardner, *Creating Minds* (Basic Books, 1993) 464 p.
4. Vera John-Steiner, *Notebooks of the Mind* (Perennial Library, 1985), 265 p.
5. Frederick Herzberg, *The Motivation to Work* (Transaction, 1993), 157 p.
6. Ralph Keeney, *Value-Focused Thinking* (Harvard), 413 p.
7. Vijay Mahajan and Robert Peterson, *Models for Innovation Diffusion* (Sage, 1985), 87 p.
8. Alex Osborn, *Applied Imagination* (Scribner's, 1963), 417 p.
9. Mark Runco, *Creativity Encyclopedia* (Academic Press, 1999) 1,693 p.
10. Mark Runco, *Divergent Thinking* (Ablex Publishing, 1991), 199 p.

III. BUSINESS AND MANAGEMENT CREATIVITY

1. Berenice Bleedorn, *The Creativity Force in Education, Business and Beyond* (Galde Press, 1998), 229 p.
2. Peter Drucker, *Innovation and Entrepreneurship: Practices and Principles* (HarperRow, 1985)
3. James Evans, *Creative Thinking In the Decision and Management Sciences* (Southwestern, 1990), 167 p.
4. Alexander Hiam, *The Manager's Pocket Guide to Creativity* (HRD Press, 1998), 180 p.
5. James Higgins, *Innovate or Evaporate: Test and Improve Your Organization's Innovation Quotient* (New Management Publishing, 1995), 400 p.
6. James Higgins, *101 Creative Problem Solving Techniques: The Handbook of New Ideas for Business* (New Management, 1994), 234 p.
7. John Kao, Jamming: *The Art and Discipline of Business Creativity* (Harper, 1997), 224 p.
8. Don Kash, *Perpetual Innovation: The New World of Competition* (Basic Books, 1989), 280 p.
9. Michael Michalko, *Thinkertoys: A Handbook of Business Creativity* (Ten Speed Press, 1991), 349 p.
10. Jerome Rosow and Robert Zager, *Productivity through Work Innovations: A Work in America Institute Policy Study* (Pergamon, 1982), 171 p.
11. Robert Zager and Michael Rosow, eds., *The Innovative Organization: Productivity Programs in Action* (Pergamon, 1982), 383 p.

IV. SCIENCE AND TECHNOLOGY CREATIVITY

1. John Diebold, *The Innovators: The Discoveries, Inventions, and Breakthroughs of Our Time* (Truman Talley Books, 1991), 316 p.
2. Michael Goldhaber, *Reinventing Technology: Policies for Democratic Values* (Routledge and Kegan Paul, 1986), 272 p.
3. Frances Karnes and Suzanne Bean, *Girls and Young Women Inventing: Twenty True Stories about Inventors* (Free Spirit, 1995), 174 p.
4. Veronica Mole and Dave Elliott, *Enterprising Innovation: An Alternative Approach* (Frances Pinter, 1987), 190 p.
5. Albert E. Muir, *The Technology Transfer System: Inventions* (Latham, 1997), 253 p.
6. Kristian Palda, *Industrial Innovation: Its Place in the Public Policy Agenda* (Fraser Institute, 1984), 232 p.
7. John Papageorgiou, *Innovation, Research-Development, and Entrepreneurship* 3, (interfaces, 1993), 66 p.

8. Virginia Postrel, *The Future and Its Enemies: The Growing Conflict Over Creativity, Enterprise, and Progress* (Free Press, 1998), 283 p.
9. Research and Technology Management Office, *Making Innovation Pay: National Innovation Workshop* (UIUC, 1997), 200 p.
10. David Roessner, *Government Innovation Policy: Design, Implementation, Evaluation* (Macmillan, 1988), 219 p.
11. Calvin Taylor and Frank Barron, eds., *Scientific Creativity: Its Recognition and Development* (Wiley, 1963), 443 p.
12. Time Magazine, *Scientists and Thinkers of the Twentieth Century* (Time-Warner, 1999), 141 p.
13. Louis Tornatzky et al., *The Process of Technological Innovation: Reviewing the Literature* (NSF, 1983), 264 p.
14. Nicholas Ziegler, *Governing Ideas: Strategies for Innovation in France and Germany* (Cornell, 1997), 266 p.
15. Harriet Zuckerman, *Scientific Elite: Nobel Laureates in the United States* (Transaction, 1996), 380 p.

V. ART, MUSIC, AND LITERATURE CREATIVITY

1. Dura Cockrell, *Introduction to Art: Theory, Practice, History* (Richard Smith, 1930), 488 p.
2. Louise Dudley and Austin Faricy, *The Humanities: Applied Aesthetics* (McGraw-Hill, 1951), 534 p.
3. Ernest Earnest, *A Foreword to Literature* (Appleton-Century, 1945), 338 p.
4. Helen Kaufman, *The Home Book of Music Appreciation* (New Home Library, 1942), 334 p.
5. Arthur Koestler, *The Act of Creation* (Macmillan, 1964), 751 p.
6. John Macy, *The Story of the World's Literature* (Liveright, 1950), 634 p.
7. Hunter Mead, *An Introduction to Aesthetics* (Ronald, 1952), 312 p.
8. Mabel Rich, *A Study of the Types of Literature* (Appleton-Century, 1937), 610 p.
9. Time Magazine, *Artists and Entertainers* (Time-Warner, 1999), 87 p.
10. Hendrik Van Loon, *The Arts* (Simon and Schuster, 1946), 700 p.

VI. PUBLIC POLICY AND ADMINISTRATION CREATIVITY

1. John Agnew, ed., *Innovation Research and Public Policy* (Syracuse, 1980), 299 p.
2. Steven Cohen and William Eimicke, *Tools for Innovators: Creative Strategies for Managing Public Sector Organizations* (Jossey-Bass, 1998), 236 p.

3. John Donahue, ed., *Making Washington Work: Tales of Innovation in the Federal Government* (Brookings, 1999), 229 p.
4. Harry Hatry et al., *Building Innovation into Program Reviews: Analysis of Service Delivery Alternatives* (Urban Institute, 1989), 122 p.
5. Patricia Ingraham and Barbara Romzek, *New Paradigms for Government: Issues for the Changing Public Service* (Jossey-Bass, 1994), 376 p.
6. Patricia Ingraham et al., eds., *Transforming Government: Lessons from the Reinvention Laboratories* (Jossey-Bass, 1998), 287 p.
7. Donald Kettl and John Dilulio, eds., *Inside the Reinvention Machine: Appraising Governmental Reform* (Brookings, 1995), 215 p.
8. Jerry Koehler and Joseph Pankowski, *Continual Improvement in Government: Tools and Methods* (St. Lucie, 1996), 158 p.
9. Russell Linden, *From Vision to Reality: Strategies of Successful Innovators in Government* (LEL, 1990), 320 p.
10. Stuart Nagel, *Creativity and Public Policy: Generating Super-Optimum Solutions* (Ashgate, 1999), 203 p.
11. David Nice, *Policy Innovation in State Government* (Iowa State, 1994), 180 p.
12. David Osborne and Ted Gaebler, *Reinventing Government: How the Entrepreneurial Spirit is Transforming the Public Sector* (Addison-Wesley, 1992), 427 p.
13. Guy Peters and Donald Savoie, (eds.), *Taking Stock: Assessing Public Sector Reforms* (McGill-Queen's University Press, 1998), 428 p.
14. Nancy Roberts and Paula King, *Transforming Public Policy: Dynamics of Policy Entrepreneurship and Innovation* (Jossey-Bass, 1996), 300 p.
15. Hindy Schachter, *Reinventing Government or Reinventing Ourselves: The Role of Citizen Owners in Making a Better Government* (SUNY Press, 1997), 148 p.

VI. PHILOSOPHY, THEORY, AND RELIGION CREATIVITY

1. Hubert Blalock, *Theory Construction: From Verbal to Mathematical Formulations* (Prentice-Hall, 1969), 191 p.
2. Charles Braden, *The World's Religions: A Short History* (Abingdon-Cokesburn Press, 1939), 256 p.
3. C. J. Ducasse, *A Philosophical Scrutiny of Religion* (Ronald, 1953), 451 p.
4. Will Durant, *The Story of Philosophy* (Garden City, 1943), 428 p.
5. Clifford Kirkpatrick, *Religion in Human Affairs* (Wiley, 1929), 543 p.
6. Nicholas Mullins, *The Art of Theory: Construction and Use* (Harper and Row, 1971), 192 p.

7. Edwin Patterson, *Jurisprudence: Men and Ideas of the Law* (Foundation, 1953), 662 p.

8. Thomas Saaty and Joyce Alexander, *Thinking with Models: Mathematical Models in the Physical, Biological and Social Sciences* (Pergamon, 1981), 192 p.

9. Arthur Stinchcombe, *Constructing Social Theories* (Harcourt, Brace, 1968), 318 p.

10. Harold Titus, *Ethics for Today* (American Book Company, 1947), 581 p.

11. Harold Titus, *Living Issues in Philosophy* (American Book, 1953), 511 p.

INDEX